Endicott Trust Company
and the Broome County Historical Society
are honored to make available
this limited edition of

THE VALLEY OF OPPORTUNITY
A Pictorial History of the Greater Binghamton Area

This is the story of the people
of the valley who worked and built this community.
Through their efforts, this region, with its cultural,
commercial, educational, industrial and charitable enterprises,
continues to be a valley of opportunity.

**Broome County
Historical Society**

Endicott Trust
Irving Bank
Corporation

THE VALLEY OF OPPORTUNITY

A Pictorial History of the Greater Binghamton Area

Gerald R. Smith

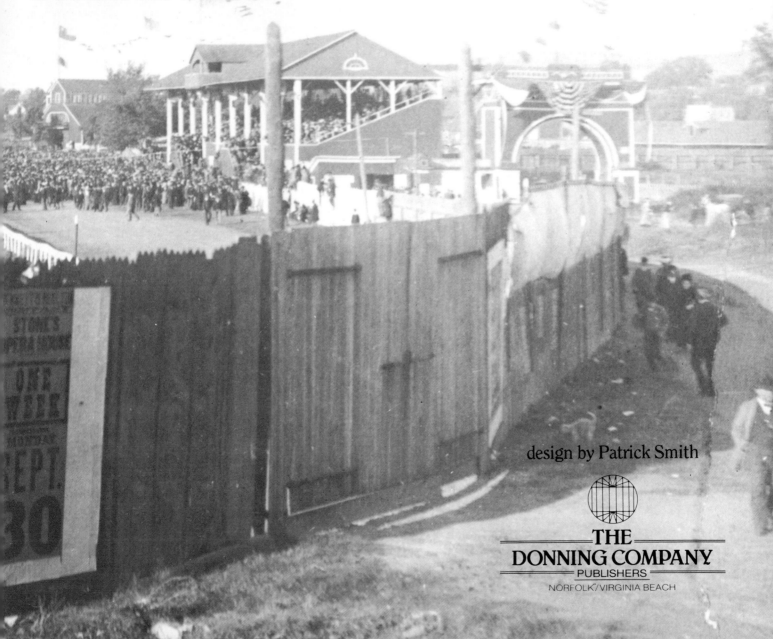

design by Patrick Smith

THE
DONNING COMPANY
PUBLISHERS
NORFOLK/VIRGINIA BEACH

Dedicated to
Kathy Mezzadonna
(1953-1985)
whose love, friendship and courage
continue to inspire me.

The Donning Company/Publishers
5659 Virginia Beach Boulevard
Norfolk, Virginia 23502

Edited by Liliane McCarthy
Richard A. Horwege, Senior Editor

Library of Congress Cataloging-in-Publication Data

Smith, Gerald R., 1954-
    The valley of opportunity.

    Bibliography: p.
    Includes index.
    1. Binghamton Region (N.Y.)—History—Pictorial works.
2. Binghamton Region (N.Y.)—Description and travel—Views. I. Title.
F129.B4S64   1988   974.7'75   88-22908
ISBN 0-89865-728-8 (lim. ed.)

Printed in the United States of America

*Cultural pursuits made significant strides as
Binghamton evolved into the Parlor City.
Women such as these began to participate in
dance recitals, local operettas, and school
plays. Courtesy of Broome County Historical
Society*

Table of Contents

Foreword 7

Preface 9

Chapter

1 The Dawn of the Valley:
   Prehistory to 1768 11

2 War, Peace, and the New Frontier:
   1768 to 1806 21

3 A Village Is Born:
   1806 to 1834 29

4 The Era of the Canal:
   1834 to 1865 35

5 The Industrial Age Cometh:
   1865 to 1880 53

6 "Segars" and the Parlor City:
   1880 to 1905 75

7 Creation of the Triple Cities:
   1905 to 1920 127

8 Partners All:
   1920 to 1941 157

9 From Smokestack to High-Tech:
   1941 to 1960 185

10 Twilight of the Valley:
    1960 to 1976 195

11 A New Day Begins:
    1976 to 1988 211

Bibliography 219

Index 220

About the Author 224

A city in transition can be seen in this photograph of Binghamton. The familiar horse and buggy was giving way to the electric trolley and the automobile, while above the streets, hundreds of electric wires brought light and power to the denizens of the Parlor City. From the Putnam Collection; courtesy of Broome County Public Library

Foreword

As the Greater Binghamton Area heads into the 1990s a healthy, vibrant community, we envision our founders in the early 1800s as a group of private individuals combining their resources to form a public partnership for the good of their flourishing community. In all likelihood, what these community pioneers did not realize is that they were establishing a tradition of public/private partnership that would last until today.

This enthusiastic little community on the confluence of the Chenango and Susquehanna rivers, combined a prime industrial location with a number of other strengths including ethnic diversity, creative problem solving, and dreams of endless prosperity. The result is a community that has developed into a "high-tech society" with no limit to its economic potential. In short, a "valley of opportunity."

City Historian Gerald R. Smith has captured the very essence of this area's rich heritage in this pictorial history of the Triple Cities. Relying on his vast knowledge of local history and his uncanny insight, Gerry has compiled a visual chronicle of this community's business and industrial developement spanning nearly two centuries. This unique publication is a significant contribution to ensuring that this area's rich heritage is concisely and accurately documented for future generations to enjoy.

Juanita M. Crabb
Mayor
City of Binghamton

The suspension bridge built in 1871 over the Chenango River connecting Clinton Street with Ferry Street (now East Clinton Street). The bridge was designed by W. A. Roebling of New Jersey, who is better known for his suspension technique on the Brooklyn Bridge.

The bridge was removed in the 1890s for a new, larger structure. The Noyes Comb factory complex can be seen in the rear of the picture. From the Putnam Collection; courtesy of Broome County Public

Preface

For a historian the writing of a pictorial history is like trying to put a jigsaw puzzle together without knowing what the puzzle is supposed to look like. As the search began for photographs, maps, and other visual materials, the premise for this book took shape. The title of a 1920 publication dealing with this area—*The Valley Of Opportunity*—was chosen because it has become synonymous with the Broome County region. It was even used by President Ronald Reagan on a stop in the area in 1984.

No single book can adequately cover all aspects of the history of an area. This book began as a companion to Lawrence Bothwell's 1983 book, *Broome County Heritage: An Illustrative History.* The focus of this volume began and continues to be the everyday people who have made this area what it is today: a good and decent place in which to live and raise a family. I wish I could have included every photograph or scene that depicts this region, but a representative sample from the nearly 20,000 pictures that were scanned for this book was chosen for inclusion in the final work. I apologize for any inadvertent error or omission that may have occurred during this selection process.

This book's creation would not have been possible without the help and assistance of many people. The constant support of the Broome County Historical Society has been of great help, and I want to especially thank Marjory Hinman, Lawrence Bothwell, and Dolores Elliott, who have read sections of the manuscript and offered valuable information and advice over these many months. The use of the extensive collections of not only the Broome County Historical Society, but also of Lawrence Bothwell, the Broome County Public Library, Your Home Library, and the Roberson Center for the Arts and Sciences, and the assistance of their staffs is sincerely appreciated. A special note of thanks goes to Bruce Wrighton, who, with few exceptions, used his considerable talents as an artist with the camera and reproduced all of the photographs used in this volume. My gratitude goes to my friends and to my co-workers at the Broome County Public Library, who have encouraged my efforts at completing this work. For my brother, Bill, who constantly pushed me as a youth to strive for higher goals, I want to express a sincere note of appreciation. Last, and never least, I want to thank my parents, Robert and Ernestine Smith, for their support, their patience, their invaluable help in editing and proofreading, and for their love, which shines in everything they do.

A depiction of early Indian life in the valley as it might have appeared around the thirteenth century. The painting by well-known local historian and artist Foster Disinger shows the Indian village whose archeological remains were discovered near the Castle Creek area in the 1930s. New data from other archeological digs in the Broome County region indicate that native inhabitants lived in the valley as early as 8000 B.C. The inhabitants of this village probably lived in longhouses, rather than the round huts shown here. Courtesy of Broome County Historical Society

Chapter One

The Dawn of the Valley
Prehistory to 1768

The sun rose slowly in the east, its rays warming the earth and welcoming another day to the valley. The clear waters of the nearby river were covered by the familiar morning mist that would evaporate shortly. In the clearing along the river's edge, the sun shown upon a group of houses. A young Indian awakened and rose to begin another day of hunting to help feed his people.

The valley had always been his home. His people had moved several times during his life, but had continually relocated along the same river. The valley provided life, not only for the Indian, but also for the animals that he hunted, and for the vegetation that was used for both food and medicine. The river that ran through the valley was a source of water for drinking and a means of transportation for the group.

The valley stretched for miles along the river, making its way southward where it widened as the river joined another, more powerful river. The valley continued westerly, and in the hills where he hunted for deer, the arrowheads of his attempts at providing meat for his people would be found centuries in the future.

The valley was a valley of opportunity for the young man. He would grow, hunt, live, love, and raise a family within a relatively small geographic area. Although he could not know it, the valley would provide those same opportunities for countless thousands during the coming centuries.

The valley that formed around the confluence of the Chenango and Susquehanna rivers was created when the glaciers of the last Ice Age receded from the land that would become New York State. The same geological movement that formed the Fingers Lakes left the southern region of the state with a series of valleys, hills and rivers, with ample varieties of flora and fauna to provide an excellent area for habitation by mankind.

The first indication of an occupation by humans in this area is between 8000 B.C. and 10,000 B.C. Although the evidence for the exact type of original population of the region is scant, the people probably hunted big game animals such as mastodons, mammoths, and elk. Archeological finds in the Broome County area indicate that several groups of people inhabited the area for the next several thousand years. Most groups consisted of hunters, fishers, and gatherers surviving off the plant and animal population in the area.

During the Woodland Period, between 1000 B.C. and contact with Europeans, the early population slowly evolved from an economy consisting of hunting, fishing, and gathering to a form of horticulture. Archeological evidence from the Endicott area indicates that a type of horticulture based on the cultivation of corn, beans, and squash was practiced at that site after A.D. 1000.

Long before any white man had journeyed through the Binghamton valley, the area was populated by several small Indian settlements. Archeological digs during the twentieth century at sites near Castle Creek and Roundtop in Endicott show Indian settlements protected by stockade-like structures. The two main local eighteenth-century settlements of Indian population were Otsiningo and Onaquaga.

These two villages were southern outposts of the Iroquois, which was mainly located in the central part of the province of New York. The League of the Five Nations (which became Six Nations after the inclusion of the Tuscaroras, circa 1722) was well developed by the early seventeenth century. The league formed a method of protection for the member nations from outside enemies and a system of keeping peace between the nations. It was also a strong factor in the French fur trading ventures in the virgin lands.

Onaquaga was a collection of small villages that formed near present-day Windsor. The larger of the two settlements, near to the Delaware River and white settlements, it was the location where the greatest amount of contact between the local Indian population, white traders, and missionaries occurred. Along the banks of the Chenango River beginning near the mouth of the Tioughnioga River in modern Chenango Forks and stretching southward to the site of Binghamton was Otsiningo, known as "the southern door of the Iroquois longhouse." Onaquaga was populated mainly by Oneida, Tuscarora, and Delaware Indians, while Otsiningo was occupied by Onondaga, Nanticoke, Shawnee, and others.

A variety of Indian agents, missionaries, and traders began to make contact with the local Indian population after 1700. The first written account of the Binghamton region was in 1737 by Conrad Weiser, who claimed that he had been here in 1726. The most prominent influence on the region was Sir William Johnson. Johnson (1715-1774) was born in Ireland and moved to the colonies in 1738 to assume the duties of managing the estate of his uncle in the lower Mohawk River valley. From this base Johnson began a trading business with the Indians and area settlers that enabled him to amass a large fortune.

During the French and Indian War, Johnson was able to use his persuasive powers to prevent the Iroquois Confederacy from supporting the French. In 1746 George Clinton, governor of the Colony of New York, appointed Johnson as colonel of the Six Nations in charge of all Indian affairs. During the remaining years of the war Johnson continued to fight the French, aiding in driving them from the colony, with the assistance of most of the Iroquois Confederacy.

After 1760 Johnson's attention was drawn to the problem of colonial settlement in a largely Indian land. Although new pioneers were moving westward in the state, most of the white population remained in the eastern portion of New York. Indians still held much of the land west of the Hudson, and it was necessary to construct a mechanism to stave off any possible conflict between the Indians and the English settlers.

In 1768 the authorities of the colony of New York, upon Johnson's planning, called the Fort Stanwix Treaty Conference. The conference was held to discuss the needs of the Indians and the problems their presence caused to the expansionist land speculators, settlers, and traders in the region. Johnson was able to provide a balanced treaty which guaranteed rights for all parties and, more importantly, established a boundary to mark the line between Indian territory and white settlement.

The line ran from Fort Stanwix (the site of modern Rome) southward along the Unadilla River to its confluence with the Susquehanna. From that point the line continued south to the Delaware River at Deposit. Both Otsiningo and Onaquaga were included in the lands established for the Indian and continued to grow in size well into the early 1770s. The treaty represented the high point in William Johnson's career. He continued to strive for better relationships with the Indian and promoted more opportunities for their educational and religious training.

Workers at the Castle Creek excavation during the 1930s gave the area its first look at the Indian population that once lived in the valley. As shown in this graphic illustration of the village found at the site, a stockade once surrounded the group of huts. Thirty years later, excavations at Roundtop near Endicott, New York, revealed evidence of early agriculture. The dating of the substances found at both sites would put them between A.D. 1000 and A.D. 1200. From William Ritchie, An Algonkin-Iroquois Contact Site on Castle Creek, Broome County, N.Y. *(1934); courtesy of Broome County Public Library*

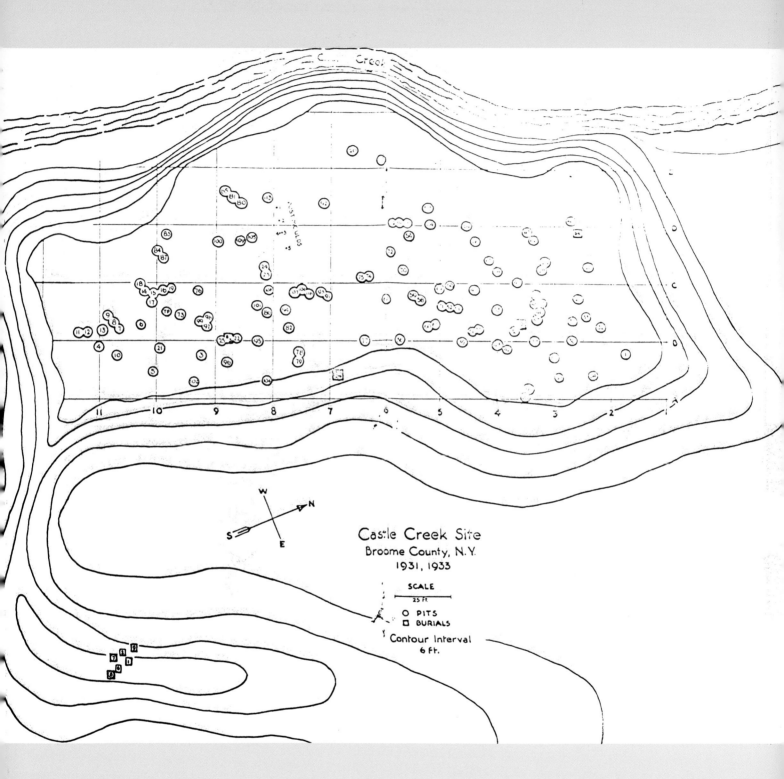

Castle Creek Site
Broome County, N.Y.
1931, 1933

SCALE
25 ft.

○ PITS
□ BURIALS

Contour Interval
6 Ft.

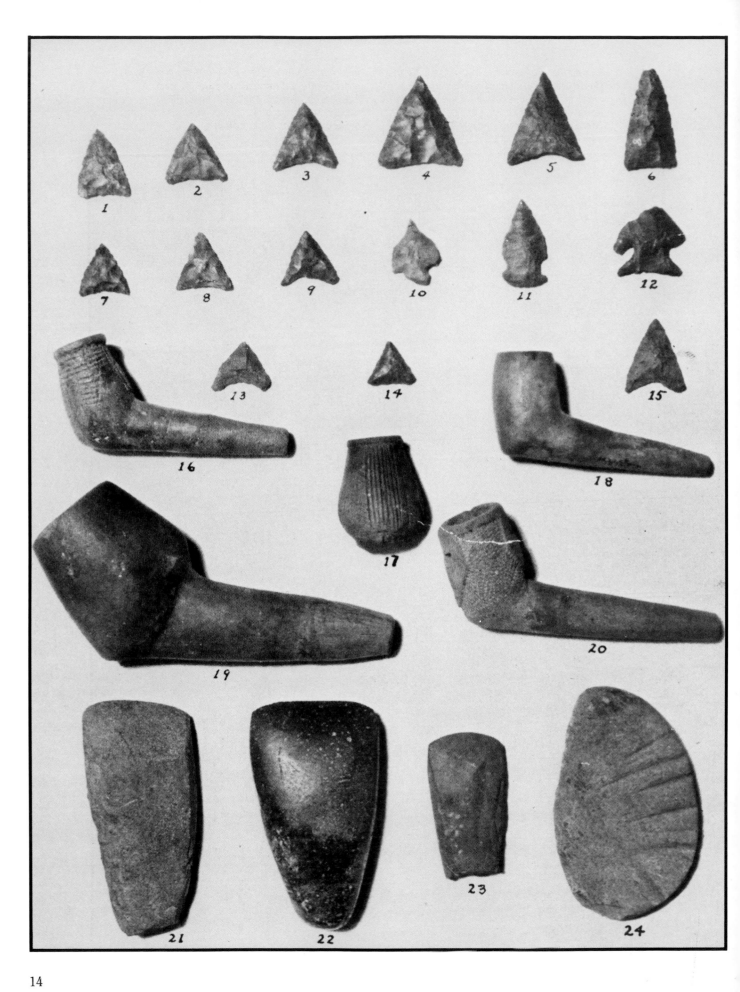

During the archeological digs of the 1930s at Castle Creek, a number of different types of artifacts were discovered. Examples of arrowheads and pottery from those digs and later excavations near the Binghamton area now reveal that the Iroquois influence began to be felt locally long before the early seventeenth century. *From William Ritchie,* An Algonkin-Iroquois Contact Site on Castle Creek, Broome County, N.Y. *(1934); courtesy of Broome County Public Library*

A pit feature from the archeological digs from the rest stop site near Otsiningo Park along Route 81. Large pits like this were found at both the Castle Creek area and the "comfort site." They were originally used as root cellars to store food such as corn and squash, and later became storage for garbage, forming small sanitary landfills. Several layers of garbage can be seen in the cut-away photograph of this pit. Courtesy of Dolores Elliott

COMFORT
W90 N70 NW
F130
6-14-72

Broome County Historian William E. Flook is shown in this 1952 photograph holding an example of some of the pottery produced by the local Indian populations. Most of these artifacts were found at the Castle Creek site. Photograph by John Warner; courtesy of Binghamton City Historian

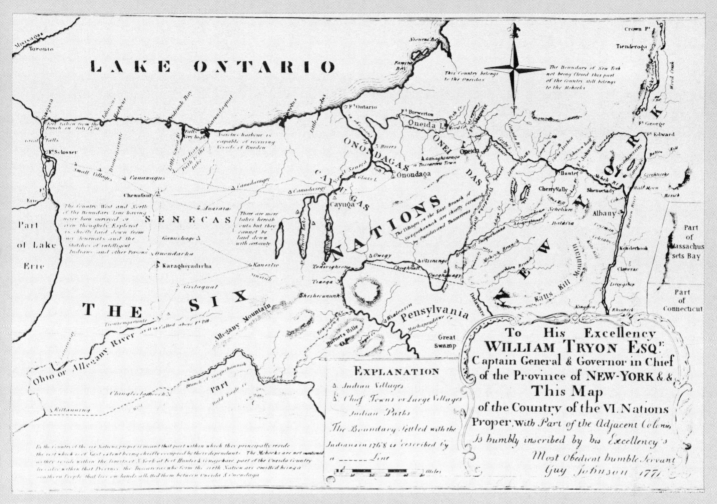

A 1771 map by Guy Johnson shows the Indian settlements in the province of New York shortly before the American Revolution. Otsiningo, along the Chenango River, and Onaquaga, near the Susquehanna River, can be seen in the center of the map. Other small settlements such as Chugnuts in the present-day town of Union also populated the Southern Tier of New York. Courtesy of Dolores Elliott

This diorama, created by Foster Disinger, depicts the arrival of Gideon Hawley at Onaquaga (also spelled Onahoquaga) on June 4, 1753. Hawley was a missionary who traveled with interpretors and guides from Stockbridge, Massachusetts, through Albany and southward to the Onaquaga site. The local Indian settlements at Ostiningo (populated mainly by Onondagas) and Onaquaga (whose inhabitants were largely Oneidas and Tuscaroras) were increasingly visited by missionaries, Indian agents, and traders after 1700. *Courtesy of Broome County Historical Society*

An engraving from 1756 depicts Sir William Johnson (1715-1774). Johnson, an Englishman who relocated to the Mohawk Valley in 1738, would become the major force in the relationship between Great Britain and the Iroquois Confederacy. His powers of persuasion brought together the British and the Indians in 1768 at Fort Stanwix to create a peaceful solution to the problem of continuing settlement by the white man and the rights of Indian nations. The settlement would be short-lived, destroyed by the American Revolution. *From* A Documentary History of New York, *vol. 2 (1849); courtesy of Binghamton City Historian*

Sʳ William Johnson Barᵗ
Major General of the English Forces
in North America.

Joseph Brant (1742-1807) was the last major Indian leader in New York State prior to the American Revolution. Descended from the Mohawk nation, Brant became a favorite of Sir William Johnson and was sent to the Eleazer Wheelock's Indian School in Lebanon, Connecticut, for education. Brant later worked as interpreter for the Reverend Charles Jeffrey Smith, a missionary who lived in Onaquaga. There Brant met his first wife

(and after her death married her half-sister).

During the American Revolution Brant and his followers supported the British side of the conflict, leading raids against the homes and supply lines of the patriots. He often used Onaquaga as a base of operations, which led to its burning by colonial forces in 1778. After the conclusion of the war Brant settled in

Canada and persuaded that government to establish lands for the Mohawk nation. This portrait of Brant first appeared in 1838 in William Stone's Life of Brant & the Border Wars (2 vols., Albany: Munsell). It is based on Ezra Ames' painting of the Indian leader (in the collection of the New York State Historical Association) and created by George Catlin, also known for Indian portraiture. Courtesy of Broome County Public Library.

Chapter Two

War, Peace and the New Frontier
1768 to 1806

Although the Fort Stanwix Treaty of 1768 seemed to have established a peaceful solution to the problem of colonial settlement, there were other forces already at work which would soon destroy Sir William Johnson's valiant effort. The League of Six Nations was a powerful force, wielding tremendous influence over all of its member nations. The leadership of that confederacy was a position of great influence. As the colonists began to focus on their grievances with Great Britain, into the role of leader of the Iroquois stepped Joseph Brant.

Brant (1742-1807) was a Mohawk whose Indian name was Thayendanegea. He had accompanied Sir William Johnson during a war campaign in 1775 and was sent to school in Lebanon, Connecticut. He worked for a time as an interpreter for a missionary who traveled near the Onaquaga area. There Brant met his first wife in 1765. She was the daughter of an Oneida chief. After her death, Brant married her half-sister. Onaquaga was an important base of operations for Brant and his supporters.

In 1775 the first shots of the American Revolution were heard at Lexington and Concord, but well before that the strained relationship between England and the colonists had begun to influence the Indian population of the valley. With the probability of war looming ever closer, both the British and the colonists were attempting to woo the sizeable Indian population to their side.

The members of the Iroquois Confederacy felt themselves splitting under the differing alliances within their group. Most of the league followed the leadership of Joseph Brant and sided with the British. There were many members of some nations, particularly the Oneida and Tuscarora, that remained faithful to the colonists' struggle. Brant took his supporters into many battles in New York, often using Onaquaga as a base of operations for his attacks on supply lines and on the homes of patriot supporters.

After Brant directed the operations that became known as the Cherry Valley Massacre in 1778, Onaquaga became the target for colonial forces. Col. William Butler led troops to that spot to rout the Indians from their homes, but upon arriving found the village already abandoned. Butler's troops destroyed the Indian town the next day and forced Brant to operate from the Deposit area and other sites.

In a major effort to prevent New York's Indians from undermining the Patriots' efforts, Gen. George Washington ordered Gen. John Sullivan and Brig. Gen. James Clinton to join forces in the region and destroy any remaining Indian bases. In the spring of 1779 the two armies began the long move to achieve this goal. Sullivan marched his troops northward through Pennsylvania toward the border of New York. Clinton's forces were already in the state and began moving southwest to meet Sullivan.

As Clinton approached the confluence of the Chenango and the Susquehanna rivers, his troops sought to destroy the local Indian villages. Since Onaquaga had been destroyed previously by Butler's forces, Otsiningo remained as the sole target. When his forces arrived, however, they found the site already burned. A few scattered Indian homes were destroyed and Clinton moved toward the west, meeting Sullivan's forces in the future Broome County at what became Union, New York.

The joint expedition successfully removed the threat by the Indian against the colonial forces. Most of the remaining Indians began to move northward, heading for Canada. In 1787 a treaty was signed in the Otsiningo area between the last local Indians and white settlers which removed the final barrier to settlement by new residents.

The open lands of the valley were like an invitation to new settlers and land speculators. People from New England and northern Pennsylvania saw the uncleared areas as an opportunity to build their own estates. Speculators saw the land as a means to amass fortunes by buying large tracts of land and selling them at a profit to eager settlers. Just north of present-day Binghamton, at the northern end of the valley, a tract of land of over 230,000 acres was sold to a number of Massachusetts speculators at twelve and one-half cents per acre, in order to settle a border dispute between that New England state and New York. The Boston Purchase formed the largest portion of the present Broome County.

The most sought-after part of the area, the site of the confluence, was granted to three individuals; Robert Hooper of New Jersey, and James Wilson and William Bingham of Pennsylvania (who formed the Canaan Land Company). In 1790 a legal settlement over the land grant split the area between the three. William Bingham received the ten-thousand-acre site at the junction of the two main rivers.

Bingham (1752-1804), a wealthy Philadelphia banker and socialite, knew that his land grant was the optimum site for a new model village. He had a vision to construct such a village, one that would be able to compete favorably with other towns in New York. In 1798 he negotiated with the recently transplanted New Englander Joshua Whitney to act as his land agent to manage his business affairs.

The main threat to the success of this venture lay with the settlement of several residents at another town just north of Bingham's lands. The continued growth of that town would impede any growth for Bingham's village. Before Whitney had an opportunity to respond to this threat he died suddenly in 1798 of Yellow Fever while on a trip in Pennsylvania. It fell upon the shoulders of his young son, Joshua, to assume the duties of land agent.

The young Joshua Whitney (1773-1845) had more ingenuity and business acumen than his father. He resolved the dilemma of the two rival villages by attending the Lewis Keeler tavern in the older village in 1800 and announcing to its patrons that a new bridge was going to be built at the confluence of the Chenango and Susquehanna at a spot marked on each bank of the Chenango River by a large elm tree. Whitney's Twin Elm story persuaded several people to move their belongings and in some cases their homes to the site of the new bridge. Although that

bridge would not be constructed until 1808, the move to the new town by the settlers ended any chance for the older village to thrive.

A new village was born on the banks of the Chenango River. By 1800 Court and Water streets were constructed, and in the same year the first newspaper, the *American Constellation*, was established. The first courthouse was built in 1802 on the northwest corner of Court and Chenango streets and later moved to a plot of land donated by William Bingham for use as a public square.

In 1801 William Bingham left America for England after the death of his wife, Anne. Although he continued to correspond with Whitney, he did not live to see the fruition of his dreams. He died in Bath, England, in 1804, never having visited the area that would bear his name.

His dream continued to grow, however. The construction of the courthouse demonstrated the rising importance of the new village of Chenango Point (as it was then called). The new town was part of Tioga County, whose county seat was located in Owego. The need for a second courthouse in the county implied that the newly settled area was forming its own political identity. On March 28, 1806, New York State created Broome County with Chenango Point as its county seat. The county, named in honor of Lt. Gov. John Broome of New York, was a new frontier with forests, rivers, and land ready to be used by the new settlers.

William Bingham (1752-1804) of Philadelphia had a vision of a new town at the confluence of the Chenango and Susquehanna rivers. A wealthy banker and land speculator, Bingham purchased over ten thousands acres in this area in 1786. His major land holdings, however, were in the state of Maine, where he owned more than three million acres. A prominent member of Pennsylvania government and early American society, he moved to England in 1801 following the death of his wife. He died there in 1804, never having seen the area that now bears his name. The original of this portrait of Bingham by Gilbert Stuart hangs in the Balch Institute in Philadelphia. A copy of the portrait can also be found in a museum on St. Christopher in the Virgin Islands, where Bingham spent two and a half years as a representative of the Continental Congress to the West Indies during the American Revolution. Courtesy of Broome County Historical Society

Anne Willing Bingham (1764-1801) was the daughter of a wealthy mercantile family from Philadelphia. Her marriage to William Bingham furthered her place among the upper-class of the fledgling nation. In diaries and correspondence of the time she is mentioned as a friend or acquaintance of the Washingtons, the Jeffersons, the Adamses, and the Madisons. Her death in 1801 was the compelling force behind her husband's relocation to Great Britian. The notation for this engraving claims that it is not a copy of the portrait of Anne Bingham by Sir Joshua Reynolds, which it closely resembles. From the Putnam Collection; courtesy of Broome County Public Library

The gravestone of Anne Bingham, located in Bermuda, where the Binghams spent much of their time in the late 1790s and early 1800s. She died there in 1801. Her Husband is buried in the Abbey in Bath, England. From the Putnam Collection; courtesy of Broome County Public Library

A MAP

OF

BINGHAM'S PATENT.

BY

G. PARK.

A legal settlement in 1790 between Robert Harpur, James Wilson, and William Bingham over a thirty-thousand-acre land patent in the southern Broome County area resulted in Bingham receiving the smallest, but best situated parcel of land. This map, drawn several

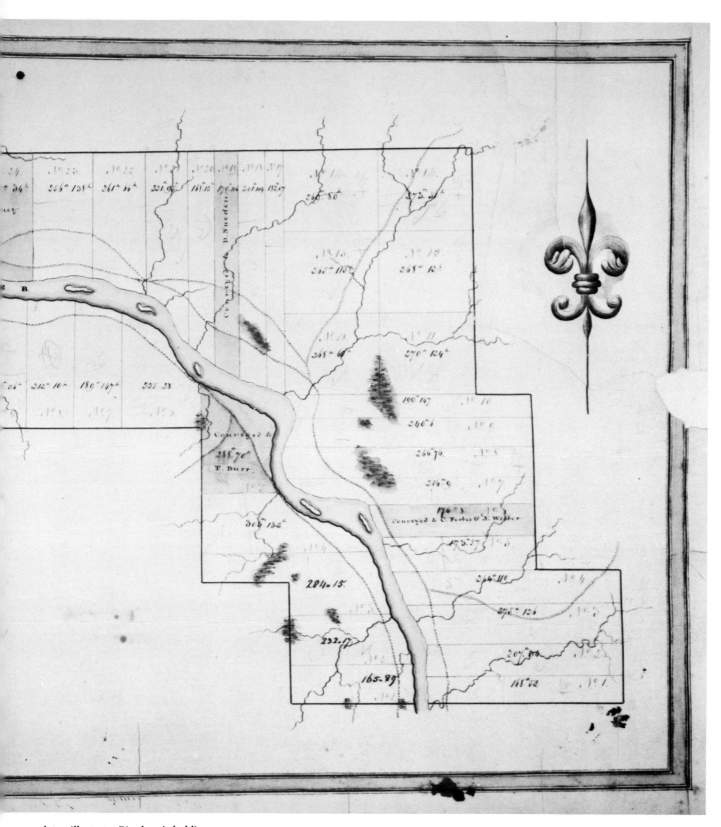

years later, illustrates Bingham's holdings. The northern boundary of Bingham's patent was used as the boundary for the city of Binghamton until 1890. Courtesy of Broome County Historical Society

This inn located in Wind Gap, Pennsylvania, was the site of the elder Joshua Whitney's death on September 26, 1798. Whitney, a native of Connecticut, moved to this area in 1787. He negotiated with William Bingham to serve as his land agent as well as maintain his general store in what is now Nimmonsburg. After the elder Whitney died from yellow fever while enroute to see Bingham, young Joshua Whitney assumed the duties of land agent for Bingham's patent in 1800. Contributed by Miss Whitney Smith, from the Putnam Collection; courtesy of Broome County Public Library

Gen. Joshua Whitney (1773-1845) as he appeared about 1838 in a portrait attributed to the well-known American artist George Catlin. Although young Whitney assumed most of his father's responsibilities after 1798, he far surpassed him in ability and power. Whitney was able to persuade the residents of Chenango Village, a rival town near present-day Nimmonsburg, that a new bridge would be constructed "at the Point," and those who wanted to be part of the new growth should move to the new lands (owned by William Bingham). It took eight years for the bridge to be built, but by then the new town of Chenango Point was well established. The General, a militia title, served two terms in the New York State legislature as this area's first representative and as county treasurer. He was a founder of Christ Church and acted as treasurer for the Chenango Bridge Company (site of the Court Street bridge). A big and powerful man (he weighed more than three hundred pounds), Whitney is considered by many to be the true founder of Binghamton. Courtesy of Broome County Historical Society

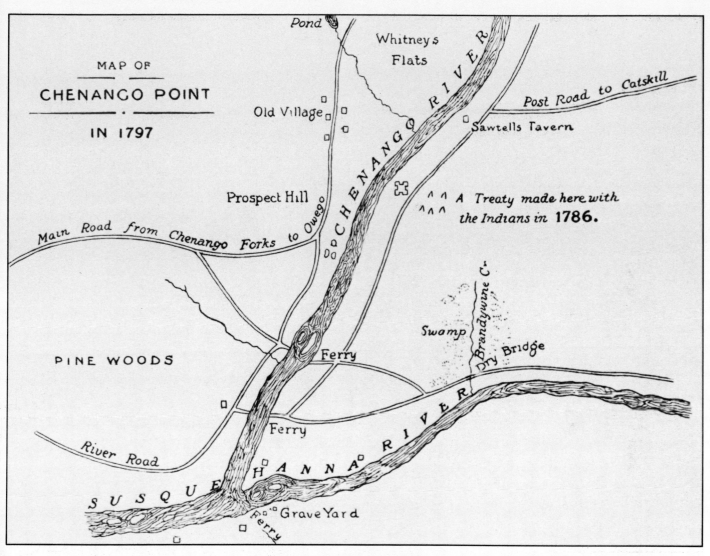

MAP OF
CHENANGO POINT
IN 1797

Pond

Whitney's Flats

Old Village

Post Road to Catskill

Sawtells Tavern

Prospect Hill

CHENANGO RIVER

Main Road from Chenango Forks to Owego

A Treaty made here with
the Indians in **1786**.

PINE WOODS

Swamp

Brandywine Cr.

Dry Bridge

Ferry

Ferry

SUSQUEHANNA RIVER

River Road

Ferry

Grave Yard

*This map of Chenango Point (later Bing-
hamton) first appeared in the 1872 reprint of
J. B. Wilkinson's* Annuals of Binghamton *of
1840. The town Chenango Village can be
seen in the upper half of the map. Joshua
Whitney's Twin Elm story of a new bridge at
the junction of the Chenango and Susquehanna rivers would result in the movement of
residents into the lands owned by William
Bingham and the expansion of the use of the
valley by the white man. Courtesy of Broome
County Historical Society*

Lt. Gov. John Broome (1734-1810) was chosen to be the namesake of the new county which split off from Tioga County in 1806. Broome served as a lieutenant colonel in the Revolutionary War, as a member of the New York State Constitutional Convention, as the first alderman of New York City, and as a member of the state assembly and senate. Broome and members of his family owned land within the county for many years. Courtesy of Broome County Historical Society

Chapter Three

A Village Is Born
1806 to 1834

The first store in the new town was erected by Judge McKinney in 1801. Within a few years, the village had a variety of shops, mercantiles, and drugstores. Many of the goods were brought to Chenango Point by turnpike or river passage. Although there was a system of turnpikes and roads connecting the town with other areas of the state, it was the rivers that became the major economic force in the community.

The process of clearing the land had created a sizable lumber industry, requiring men to clear the land, build sawmills, and construct rafts to carry goods along the Chenango and Susquehanna rivers and their tributaries. These rivers provided farmers with a means to transport and sell goods to merchants in Binghamton (as the new village would be called). Local agriculture improved from a subsistance level to a profitable venture, with the manufacture of lath strips, shingles, barrels, and potash on a small scale by many farmers.

To the west of Binghamton the towns of Union and Vestal saw the arrival of settlers from New England and Pennsylvania, who began to build homesteads on the open land. The population of Binghamton increased from about three hundred in 1812 to two thousand in 1840, while the county's population increased 350 percent in the same time period.

The arrival of increasing numbers of persons created other needs for the village. In 1828 a second courthouse was constructed. Improvement in the use of the rivers was sought by many residents. The local rivers provided a method for economic opportunity, but the level of water in those rivers and streams fluctuated greatly, and the use of rafts to transport goods could be extremely slow. It was not uncommon for finished lumber or other goods to take over a month to be delivered to sites outside of the area. A better system needed to be developed to improve water transportation and remove the new village from relative isolation within the state.

The search for the new system turned toward the development of a canal in the region. Through the leadership of George Clinton, the Erie Canal opened in 1825. It successfully connected the western portions of New York to the eastern half of the state and to the Hudson River. Immediately after the canal opened many residents of the state caught "canal fever," rushing to pass legislation authorizing the construction of canals in several areas of New York.

In Binghamton the struggle for a canal was long and arduous. The initial legislation for a canal passed in the New York State legislature in 1829. The difficulty was in the selection of the northern terminus for the canal. In 1834 Utica was finally selected (after much political maneuvering) as the point at which the canal would connect with the Erie Canal. It would be three more years before the new system would open.

At the same time as arguments over the canal were proceeding in Albany, the town of Binghamton was legally incorporated as a village on May 3, 1834. On June 4 of that year several residents met at Peterson's Tavern (located near the bridge over the Chenango River) to establish Binghamton's first government. The village was divided into five wards, and the young Daniel S. Dickinson, a newly arrived attorney, was chosen as its first president. The rapid rise of the new village, the increasing population in the surrounding area, and the promise of a new transportation system left the valley on the edge of a great future.

Two views of Joshua Whitney's home on Court Street, near the present-day Alice Street. Whitney intended his home, constructed in 1806, to be a showplace. The photograph, shown on this page, shows the exterior and grounds as they appeared in the mid-nineteenth century. The photograph, shown on next page, was taken in 1915 by Dr. H. Q. Ely shortly before the home's demolition to make way for expansion on Binghamton's east side. Photograph, on page 30, courtesy of Broome County Historical Society. Photograph on page 31, the Putnam Collection, courtesy of Broome County Public Library

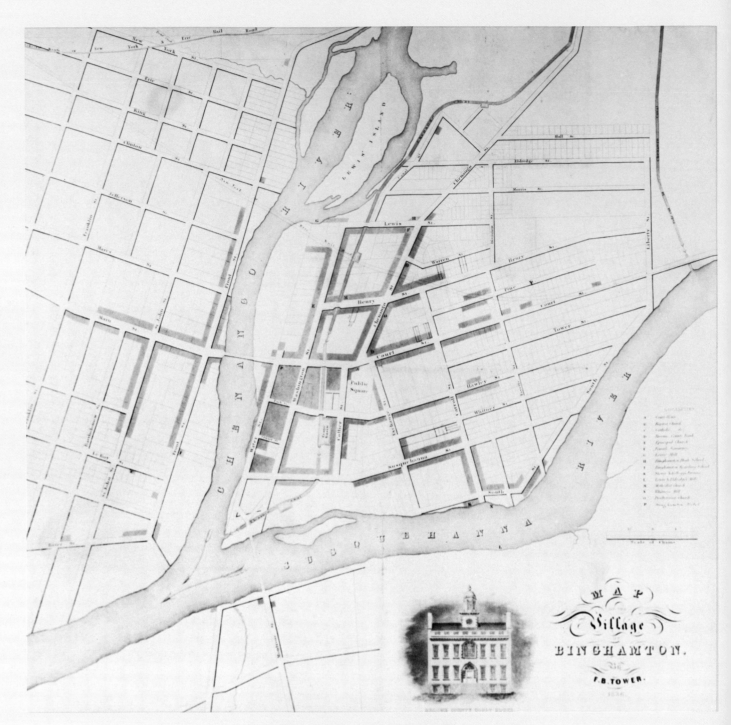

F. B. Tower's father was a local merchant
operating in the village of Binghamton. The
son is better remembered for his 1836 map of
Binghamton. The map shows a new urban
area, with the street plan completed and a
population centered near the confluence of
the two rivers, ready for rapid growth. Courtesy of Broome County Historical Society

This detail from F.B. Tower's 1836 map of the village of Binghamton shows the second Broome County Courthouse, which was constructed in 1830. The building was constructed of brick and stood on the northern edge of the public square facing the Chenango River. The jail was housed in the basement of the structure. Courtesy of Broome County Historical Society

On May 3, 1834, New York State passed an act of incorporation for the new village of Binghamton. Four weeks later, on June 4, several of the most important residents of that village met at Samuel Peterson's Tavern (shown here) on the corner of Front and Main streets to establish the first government.

Binghamton was divided into five wards (it now has thirteen), and Daniel S. Dickinson, an attorney who had moved to the area only four years earlier, was chosen to be the village's first president. Until new village offices could be constructed, the inn was used as the home of the village's government. Peterson's

Tavern was a popular stage coach stop during the first half of the nineteenth century. The tavern burned in 1859. The site is now occupied by the First Congregational Church. Painting by Edward F. Dibble; original owned by the First Congregational Church; miniature courtesy of Binghamton City Historian

An early photograph of Ingleside, the home of John A. Collier. An attorney who located in Binghamton in 1809, Collier was an influential member of the community. He went into partnership with Daniel LeRoy and served as this community's district attorney, as a partner in a river navigation company, and as the first representative from Broome County to serve in the United States Congress. Ingleside was constructed in 1837 at the corner of Prospect and Eldridge streets. The western side of the estate faced the Chenango Canal. From the Putnam Collection; courtesy of Broome County Public Library

Chapter Four

The Era of the Canal
1834 to 1865

On May 6, 1837, the first boat on the Chenango Canal arrived in Binghamton, signifying the connection between Binghamton, Utica, and the Erie Canal. During the previous three years of canal construction, a system of locks ninety-five miles long and forty-six feet wide that followed the route of the Chenango River was created. The opening of the Chenango Canal meant the establishment of a reliable means of transportation that would promote the rapid growth Binghamton of business and lumbering in the region.

The success of the canal brought larger numbers of people into the valley. Significant numbers of immigrants from Ireland and Germany settled in Broome County during the 1840s. Nearly twelve thousand new residents arrived between the opening of the canal and the outbreak of the Civil War. These immigrants provided the region with a valuable source of labor for the growing industrial base.

The early education system was not adequate to handle the large numbers of children that needed schooling. Private academies, such as the Binghamton Academy and the Susquehanna Seminary, arose to fill that gap. In 1861 New York State passed the Union Free School Act, which established a series of free schools throughout the state. Although the private academies would survive for many more years, the union schools became increasingly popular.

Religious groups had begun to establish churches in the area as far back as the 1790s, but these early attempts failed, and it was not until the early 1800s that the region saw any Protestant churches firmly anchored in the area. The arrival of immigrants promoted a diversification of the type of churches this area could support. By the late 1830s the first Catholic church, Saint John's Church, and two black churches had opened their doors to new congregations.

Even before the Chenango Canal was completed, there appeared a new type of transportation which treatened the canal's very existence—the railroad. The history of the "iron horse" dates to 1822 with the creation of the New York and Erie Railroad. Three prominent local citizens—Daniel Dickinson, Stephen Weed, and Amni Doubleday—established the Binghamton and Susquehanna Railroad Company in 1833. Two years later the Erie Railroad began construction on an east-west railroad across the state. In December 1848 the first train arrived in Binghamton, its whistle signifying the beginning of the end for the Chenango Canal.

The canal, like all other canals in New York, never made a profit (only the Erie was profitable). Although it provided a valuable means of transporting goods, it was too slow to compete against the speed of the railroad. In an effort at making the canal an attractive and viable system, plans were made to extend the end of the canal from Binghamton westward, following the route of the Susquehanna River until it connected with the canal system of Pennsylvania. Approval for this extension was finally granted in 1864, and some expansion was begun.

The Binghamton valley was gradually pulled into the political maelstrom that existed in the nation during the second quarter of the nineteenth century. The country was in the depths of a fight concerning the issues of slavery and states' rights. Daniel S. Dickinson, former Binghamton Village president, now represented New York in the United States Senate (1844-1851). He became an important supporter of the Compromise of 1850, and advocated compromise, hoping it would allow the "peculiar institution" of slavery to eventually fade away.

Despite the efforts of Dickinson and other leading politicians, neither the Compromise of 1850 nor other efforts could stave off the inevitable conflict. The nation was thrown into a civil war, and the call to arms by Abraham Lincoln was answered by many local residents. The canal and the railroads were used to transport goods and men to the battlefronts and to return the dead to their families. In the town of Union a sawmill was given a contract to cut lumber for a low ship that could bear both ironclads and armaments to fight naval battles. That mill, with its surrounding mill houses for its workers, which provided the required lumber for the *Monitor,* would later become the site of the area's largest shopping center, the Oakdale Mall.

With the conclusion of the Civil War, the nation began the long process of healing its wounds. In the valley, the conflict had had a profound effect. The technology needed to arm the nation and to transport the goods and the men to battle had become the means of catapulting this area into the period of its largest growth.

The Collier mansion as it appeared in 1924. The columns on the east and west sides of the home had been removed and the surrounding lands sold for commercial development. The structure was used for many years as a gas station and was demolished in 1967. Today, the area used for apartment buildings and light industries, is in the process of rehabilitation. From the Putnam Collection; courtesy of Broome County Public Library

The announcement in 1833 of the passage of an act authorizing the construction of the Chenango Canal was the culmination of nearly four years of work. It was another year before ground was broken. The canal opened in the spring of 1837 and ran from Utica in the north (the original terminus was to have been Whitesboro) to Binghamton in the south. The canal was ninety-five miles long and cost close to two million dollars. This broadside dates from 1838. Courtesy of Broome County Historical Society

CHENANGO CANAL.

STORAGE

AND

FORWARDING.

The subscriber having taken the large and commodious WARE-HOUSE, recently erected in this village by Charles M'Kinney, takes this method to inform the public, that he is prepared to receive any description of property, to be transported to any point on the *Chenango & Erie Canals*, and also to receive goods on Storage.

Merchants and others receiving goods by the

Canal Boats,

will find it their interest to patronize the subscriber, as the Storehouse is more conveniently located than any other in the village, being immediately above the Lock, north of Court street.

All property stored with the subscriber for transportation, will be forwarded in the first Boat, and strictly according to order.

Punctual attendance will be given at all hours, and charges as reasonable as at any other establishment·

JOHN C. ROBINSON.

Binghamton, September, 1838.

COURIER OFFICE, BINGHAMTON

Looking toward the west, this mid-nineteenth century photograph shows a portion of the Chenango Canal in Binghamton. Intersecting Court Street at what is today State Street, the canal was crossed by "the iron bridge." The dome of the third courthouse can be seen on the left. From the Putnam Collection; Courtesy of Broome County Public Library

The opening of the canal dramatically affected the economy of the Binghamton area. New stores, hotels, and industries began or moved to the area to prosper from "canal fever." This view of Court Street, taken about 1840 near the canal, shows the expansion of businesses along the length of the village's main thoroughfare. The Phoenix Hotel, later called the Exchange Hotel, can be seen in the center of the photograph. It was replaced by Woolworth's in 1949. Courtesy of Broome County Historical Society

One of the area's most famous retail stores began as a result of the canal's opening, which provided a viable means of bringing goods to the area for sale to local residents. This detail from an 1855 map of Broome County shows "the iron bridge" over the canal next to Sisson Brothers and Weldon Store. The store continued in operation until the early 1960s. Courtesy of Broome County Historical Society

The Chenango Canal brought change for not only Binghamton, but also for other areas in the valley. This coal station was located along the canal route in Port Dickinson. Both Port Dickinson and Port Crane were named because of the canal route through those two areas. The distinct shape of a canal packet boat can be seen on the right-hand side of the photograph, near the building adjacent to the canal. The Syracuse and Binghamton Railroad, which opened in 1854, runs next to the canal. From the Putnam Collection; courtesy of Broome County Public Library

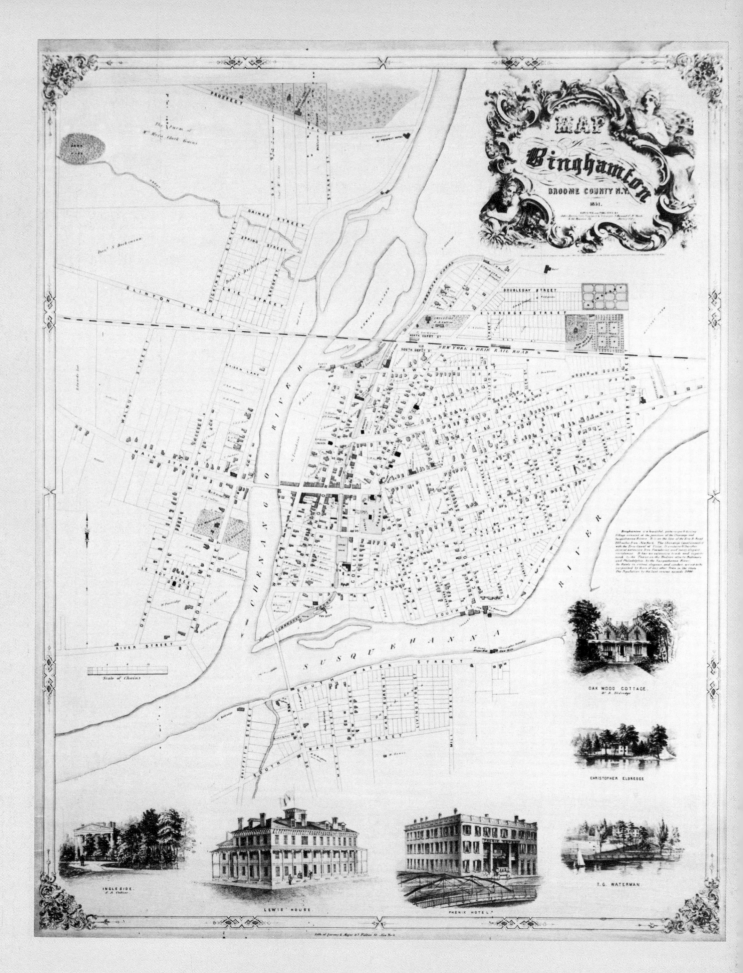

MAP of Binghamton

BROOME COUNTY N.Y.
1851.

OAK WOOD COTTAGE.

CHRISTOPHER ELDREDGE

INGLESIDE.

LEWIS' HOUSE

PHENIX HOTEL.

T.G. WATERMAN

OAK WOOD COTTAGE.
Dr E. Eldredge

*An 1851 map of the village of Binghamton by
John Bevan illustrates the expansion of business throughout the downtown section; the
population by the mid-nineteenth century
had begun to expand towards the west. The
detail shows Oakwood Cottage, home of Dr.
Edwin Eldredge, located on Eldredge Street
until demolished for railroad expansion.
Courtesy of Broome County Historical Society*

Originally from Goshen, Connecticut, Daniel S. Dickinson (1800-1866) Moved to Binghamton from Chenango County in 1831 after becoming an attorney. He was the village's first president and served in the state senate from 1837 to 1840. He was elected lieutenant governor in 1842 and replaced Senator Talmadge in the United States Senate in 1844. He was elected to a six-year term ending in 1850. As a Democrat, Dickinson strongly believed in states' rights and became a leader in the formation and ratification of the Compromise of 1850. Although efforts were made to nominate him for president at the Democratic Convention in 1852, Dickinson chose not to seek the office. During the Civil War, Dickinson spoke tirelessly in many states in support of the union. His estate, the Orchard, included much of the First Ward of Binghamton. He died in New York City in 1866 shortly after his appointment as United States district attorney for the Southern District of New York. Courtesy of Broome County Historical Society

The oldest standing church building in the Triple Cities, Christ Church was constructed in 1854. It was designed by Richard Upjohn and the steeple, although included in the original plans, was not completed until 1903. Courtesy of Broome County Historical Society

Many other religions established churches in the valley shortly after the beginning of the nineteenth century. The original Baptist Church dates to 1829, while the First Baptist Church on Chenango Street, seen in this photograph, was opened in 1893. It was torn down in the 1970s to make way for 100 Chenango Place. Courtesy of Broome County Historical Society

In 1838 St. John's Catholic Church opened on Leroy Street. In 1873 the present church (seen in this 1890 photograph) was constructed on the same site and renamed St. Patrick's Church. Two black churches, the Bethel Church and the First Colored M. E. Zion Chapel, were also incorporated in 1838, and continue in reorganized form today. From Binghamton Illustrated; courtesy of Binghamton City Historian

In 1835 Dr. Stephen D. Hand (1806-1879) came to Binghamton from New Lebanon, New York. He had received his medical degree from Williams College and swiftly established a sizable practice in the new village. He was president of the Broome County Medical Society from 1840 to 1842, during which time he spoke fervently against the homeopathic medical field that was becoming increasingly popular in the mid-nineteenth century.

He was active in the "underground railroad" efforts prior to the outbreak of the Civil War, using his home as a station along that "line" (as well as possible sites at Christ Church and both black churches in the village). Hand began to use some of the techniques of homeopathic medicine and within a short time converted exclusively to homeopathy. He again attracted many followers, and became president of the Broome County Homeopathic Medical Society in 1863. He continued to practice this form of medicine until his death at age 73. Courtesy of Broome County Historical Society

The Blanchard and Bartlett Planing Mill can be seen in the foreground of this picture. The mill was located near the corner of present-day Hawley and Collier streets, and exemplifies the transformation from subsistence cottage-type work to an organized industrial effort. The lumber industry played a dominant role in local business in the early nineteenth century, but by the 1860s the industry was responding to a need for finished lumber and furniture. The Bartlett Mill was adjacent to the Chenango Canal, enabling the mill to bring in unfinished lumber and ship finished goods to many markets. The covered bridge at Washington Street is in the upper-center of the photograph. From the Putnam Collection; courtesy of Broome County Public Library

Taken from the courthouse, this photograph of Binghamton shows the growing village in 1856. The intersection of Court Street in the foreground and Chenango Street in the center of the picture can be seen. The southwest corner of Chenango Street has been occupied by a bank since the 1840s. Visible on the corner in this view is the Morgan House. The familiar shape of Christ Church can be found in the center-left of the scene. Courtesy of the Broome County Historical Society

The employees of the Blanchard and Bartlett Planing Mill in a photograph taken about 1860. The work force of the plant was exclusively male, with a small percentage of child labor—typical of the use of labor in the mid-nineteenth century. The changes in the industrial structure in the country would forever alter the makeup of the work force in the next half century. From the Putnam Collection; courtesy of Broome County Public Library

1865 DAILY 1865
PACKET LINE
BETWEEN

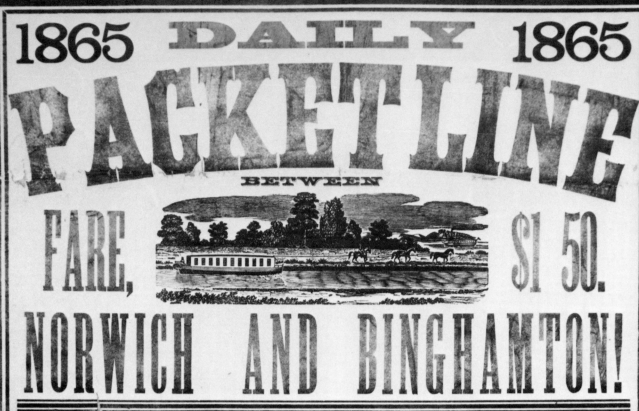

FARE, $1 50.
NORWICH AND BINGHAMTON!

The Lillie!
CAPT. WM. STEVER,

Leaves Norwich, Monday, Wednesday and Friday, at 6 a. m., Oxford, 8 a. m., East Greene, 10.30 a. m., Greene, 12 M., Chenango Forks, 2 p. m., and Port Crane, at 4 p. m., arriving at Binghamton at 6 p. m., the Packet Norwich, alternating with the Lillie, on the same time table, Tuesdays, Thursdays and Saturdays.

The Norwich!
Capt. Henry T. Stever,

Leaves Binghamton, Monday, Wednesday and Friday at 6 a. m., Port Crane, 8 a. m., Chenango Forks, 10 a. m., Greene 12 M., East Greene, 1.30 p. m., Oxford, 4 p. m., arriving at Norwich at 6.30 p. m., the Packet Lillie, alternating with the Norwich, on the same time table, Tuesdays, Thursdays and Saturdays.

PACKAGES AND FREIGHT!

All PACKAGES designed for this line of Boats should be Marked " *Via* PACKET," or " CARE of the respective Captains."   All articles so marked and entrusted to their care, will receive the strictest attention.

Travelers favoring this line with their patronage will, when desired, be served with meals at regular hours, and polite attention given to their comfort, these boats having been fitted up in the most approved modern style, for passengers.

NORWICH, September 16, 1865.   J. L. BURTIS, Job Printer, Democrat Office, Oxford, N. Y.

This is the mill that was located on the Susquehanna River next to Conklin Avenue and near present-day Mill Street. The area's water power was a significant factor in the development of many small industries on both banks of this river at Rockbottom Dam in an area of Binghamton known as Millsville. This circa 1860 photograph also shows the covered bridge which spanned the river near the dam. Courtesy of Broome County Historical Society

An interesting view of nineteenth-century advertising techniques can be seen in this photograph. The standard with the top hat clearly marked the type of business located in the building. Chollar's hat shop was located in Binghamton, on Court Street. The advertising card notes that the horse and wagon belonged to Joe Short. From the Putnam Collection; courtesy of Broome County Public Library

The notation on the back of one photograph of this building mistakenly calls this the Female Seminary. This was the Binghamton Academy, which was incorporated by New York State in 1842. It was located on Courthouse Square, in the rear of the courthouse (just north of the present-day Justice Building). The basement was used as a residence for the academy's principal. The school operated until 1861, and the building was torn down in 1864. Courtesy of Broome County Historical Society

Binghamton Daily Republican--Extra.

THE STARS AND STRIPES STILL WAVE From the Battlements of FORT SUMTER!!

By Telegraph.

FOR THE BINGHAMTON DAILY REPUBLICAN.

Reported by the
SYRACUSE AND BINGHAMTON, and
NEW YORK & ERIE RAILROAD TELEGRAPH LINES.

CHARLESTON, Saturday, April 13,
12 o'clock, noon.

The ships in the offing appear to be quietly at anchor. They have not fired a gun.

The entire roof of the barracks at Fort Sumter are in a vast sheet of flame. Federal flag still waves. Major Anderson is occupied in putting out the fire.

CHARLESTON, April 13, 1:30 p. m.

The batteries on Sullivan's Island and Cummings' Point, and Stevens' Battery are pouring shot and shell into Fort Sumter.

Major Anderson does not return the fire.

Maj. A. has blown up one or two buildings to arrest the flames. This does not in any wise diminish his strength. He has been compelled to cease firing altogether.

The ships outside are supposed to inaugurate the blockade.

Major Anderson's flag has been shot away, and now waves from a pole on the ramparts.

It is reported that Major Anderson is blowing up the casements seaward, with a view to escape in boats during the night.

Offers have been received from Virginia of any number of men required for fighting duty.

Major Anderson has thrown out a raft loaded with men who are dipping up buckets of water, to extinguish the fire.

The fort is scarcely discernable. The men on the raft are now objects of fire from Morris Island. With good glasses, the balls can be seen skipping over the water and striking the unprotected raft. Great havoc is created amongst the poor fellows.

At half past eleven o'clock the flames were bursting from all the port-holes. The destruction of Fort Sumter is inevitable.

CHARLESTON, April 13.

It is stated from a reliable source that up to 10 o'clock to-day no one at Fort Moultrie was killed.

Eleven shots from Fort Sumter penetrated the Floating Battery below the water line.

The few shots fired by Major Anderson this morning knocked the chimneys from the officer's quarters at Fort Moultrie like a whirlwind.

Major Anderson's only hope now is to hold out for aid from the ships.

Two ships are making in towards Morris Island, with a view to land troops and silence the batteries there.

Four vessels, two of them large steamers, are in sight over the bar.

The largest appears to be engaging Morris Island.

The flames have nearly subsided in Sumter, but Major Anderson does not fire any guns.

General Beauregard left the wharf just now in a boat for Morris Island.

☞ It is reported that leading Ohio Democrats have sent this dispatch to the President: "We are with you to the death, if you will hold Fort Sumter. The necessity of holding it is absolute."

☞ It is understood that Gov. Curtin, of Pennsylvania, will order out the Militia of the State on the first sign of danger to the Capital. It would require but a single unprovoked shot from a Southern Battery to make a million of freemen ready to volunteer for the defence of the Union.—[Albany Journal.

On April 12, 1861, Fort Sumter, located off the South Carolina coast, was fired upon by forces led by Gen. Pierre G. T. Beauregard, and the Civil War began. This announcement of the event appeared in the Binghamton Daily Republican, and soon after the call went out throughout the region for volunteers to put down the uprising. Courtesy of Broome County Historical Society

CONKLIN TO THE RESCUE!

DICKINSON GUARD!

The undersigned having received the proper authority, proposes to form, from those desiring to serve their Country, in this and adjoining sections of country, a Company of Light Infantry for the Regiment which Hon. D. S. DICKINSON has been authorized to raise by the Secretary of War---the Regiment to be styled the

DICKINSON GUARD!

"No fearing, no doubting a Soldier should know,
When here stands his country and yonder the foe ;
One look at the bright sun, one prayer to the sky,
One glance to where our starry-flag floats glorious on high ;
Then on, as the young lion bounds on his prey---
Let the sword flash on high---fling the scabbard away !"

☞ Those who wish to join the Regiment are invited to call on the undersigned at CORBETTSVILLE, and enter their names.

FRANK BURT.

CORBETTSVILLE, Sept. 19, 1861.

The call to arms during the Civil War did not go unheeded. Over four thousand men from Broome County voluntarily served in thirteen different regiments during the four years of the conflict. The Dickinson Guard, which formed in the town of Conklin in 1861, was named after local politician Daniel S. Dickinson. Courtesy of Broome County Historical Society

A vivid reminder of the Civil War, the unidentified veteran of the War Between the States stands next to a young child during the first celebration of Veteran's Day in the area in 1926. Courtesy of Broome County Historical Society

The arrival of the "iron horse" brought many changes for the people of the valley. The Erie Railroad began construction in the county in 1835 near Deposit. The railroad completed its east-west line in 1851. The north-south line of the Delaware and Hudson was not opened until January 12, 1869. Binghamton and the surrounding villages were finally connected to the rest of the nation. The crew of an early locomotive can be seen in this photograph. Courtesy of Broome County Historical Society

Chapter Five

The Industrial Age Cometh
1865 to 1880

While the southern half of the country was embroiled in the throes of Reconstruction, the valley surrounding Binghamton was in a very different type of metamorphosis. The development of a railroad system that included both north-south lines and east-west lines allowed Binghamton and the surrounding townships to be connected to other areas throughout the United States. For the first time, the area had a means of transportation that would allow large amounts of raw materials to be shipped into the area and finished goods to be shipped out to both national and international markets.

The population of the village of Binghamton had grown to over ten thousand persons by 1865. On April 9, 1867, thirty-four years after its incorporation as a village, Binghamton became a city. Abel Bennett, a local businessman, was selected to be the city's first mayor. The upgrading to city status was only one of many changes during the next two decades that helped to improve the quality of life for the area's residents.

The region's first telegraph office opened in 1863, and a third, larger courthouse was constructed by 1857. The move toward philanthropic efforts began with the establishment of groups such as the Young Men's Christian Association (1865) and the New York State Inebriate Asylum (1858), which would become the Binghamton Asylum for the Chronic Insane in 1879. The first horse-drawn railway, the Binghamton and Port Dickinson Company, began services in 1868, and in the same year the city saw its first sewer system completed. The beginnings of a park system took form with the donation of Ross Park to the city in 1875. Nearby the village of Union was incorporated in 1871.

The most significant change was in the industrial structure of the area. Industries that had been the staple of the area's economy either disappeared entirely or were transformed into a related field. While the lumber industry did not cease operating during this time, the emphasis moved toward finished goods, such as furniture and wagon and carriage manufacture. New firms concerned with the production of standardized parts used in the manufacture of farm equipment began, and an industry involved with the tanning of leather and production of finished leather goods took form. In 1858 the first cigar factory in Binghamton opened. It was a symbol of the industry that would lead the region into the next century.

Despite valiant efforts in the 1860s to resurrect the Chenango Canal, by the 1870s use of the facility had all but ended. Much of the canal lay in disrepair, and by 1875 the canal was closed and the locks were filled and sold to the city to be used for the construction of State Street.

Binghamton was slowly moving away from the small backwoods village, and was adopting many of the services and features of a modern city. More and more people were now residing on the lands to the west of the city.

The people of the valley had survived the horrors of terrible bloodshed and learned to use the technologies of war to move ahead. The last quarter of the century quickly approached, and the promise of even greater growth was at hand.

In April 1866 Daniel S. Dickinson, former United States senator from New York, died in New York City. His death was commemorated by elaborate bunting on the courthouse. This photograph shows the third Broome County Courthouse, constructed on the public square in 1858. It was the first courthouse to face the Court Street Chenango Street intersection, rather than the Court Street bridge. The County clerk's office was located in a separate building, seen in the lower right-hand side of the picture. From the Putnam Collection; courtesy of Broome County Public Library

This was Broome County's first separate jail building. It was located in the rear of the courthouse and was constructed in 1858. The complex included both a jail and a home for the sheriff. Courtesy of Broome County Historical Society

On April 9, 1867, Binghamton was incorporated as a city. Binghamton had grown substantially in the thirty-three years since it had become a village. The population had grown from two thousand to over ten thousand. In May 1867 the city's first mayoral election was held. Abel Bennett (shown), a Republican, was the victor over Samuel Hall. Bennett was a leading businessman in the city. He owned and operated the Hotel Bennett on Water Street. The original of this portrait of Bennett hung for many years in City Council Chambers in old City Hall. Courtesy of Broome County Historical Society

Fireman's Hall was built in 1857 on Collier Street to house the fire company and the village headquarters. This stereoscopic view from 1865 indicates the jubilation at the end of the Civil War. The building was removed in 1896 to make way for the new City Hall building. Courtesy of Broome County Historical Society

The tollhouse and covered bridge over the Susquehanna River near present-day South Washington Street. The tollkeeper also used the building for a residence. The bridge was constructed in 1843 and was 700 feet long. It removed in the 1880s when the current span was constructed. From the Putnam Collection; courtesy of Broome County Public Library

One of the more prominent veterans to emerge from the Civil War was Gen. Edward F. Jones. After returning from the war, Jones began a scale manufacturing business with about twenty men. Within a short time the quality of the scale became well known and business increased significantly. The company eventually employed three hundred men in a plant in the First Ward near the former Daniel Dickinson School. The phrase "Jones, He Pays the Freight" became synonymous with the firm. After Jones' death in 1913 the firm became a division of the Consolidated Utilities Corporation. It closed in the early 1920s. Courtesy of Broome County Historical Society

SCALE DIVISION
OF
CONSOLIDATED UTILITIES CORPORATION

ANNOUNCEMENT

of the Consolidation of

JONES OF BINGHAMTON CO., Inc.
"JONES, HE PAYS THE FREIGHT"
Binghamton, N. Y.
Scale Works

OSGOOD SCALE DIVISION
Binghamton, N. Y.
Scale Manufacturers

EMCO MANUFACTURING CO., Inc.
Binghamton, N. Y.
Automobile Accessories

WOODWORTH MANUFACTURING CORPORATION
Niagara Falls, N. Y., Niagara Falls, Ont.
Automobile Accessories

A Big New Force Toward Binghamton's Future Growth

CONSOLIDATED UTILITIES CORPORATION
BINGHAMTON, NEW YORK   ::   ::   ::   U. S. A.

Advertisement announcing the consolidation of Jones of Binghamton with Consolidated Utilities. Courtesy of Broome County Historical Society

The Harmony Seminary was a private school
for the instruction of young ladies which was
located on Chenango Street. The school
began operations in 1842 and constructed its
second building in 1851. Many members of
the Marsh family instructed the school's
pupils. As many as five hundred students
passed through this school's halls. From the
Putnam Collection; courtesy of Broome
County Public Library

While the majority of Broome County's population was centered in Binghamton during the last half of the nineteenth century, the western areas of the county were also developing. Businesses and people began to move to the towns of Vestal and Union. The J. L. Rounds estate, seen in this engraving from Everts, Ensign and Everts 1876 Broome County atlas, was located near the Susquehanna River crossing to Union. The home originally opened as an inn in the 1840s and later was used as a residence and as apartments. It reopened as Drover's Inn in 1987. Courtesy of Broome County Historical Society

The spread of industry and population followed the lines of the railroads. Stops along the lines brought a need for hotels and restaurants in outlying areas in the valley. In 1852 Maj. David Mercereau built the Major House hotel in the village of Union. This photograph dates from the late nineteenth century, when the hotel was still in operation. Courtesy of Broome County Historical Society

BINGHAMTON WATER CURE,

BINGHAMTON, BROOME COUNTY, N. Y.

This Institution was established in Binghamton in 1849, since which time it has treated successfully thousands of invalids.

The Cure is beautifully situated on the side of Mt. Prospect, surrounded by large trees, and commanding a fine view of the city, rivers, hills, and the magnificent scenery in the immediate vicinity, and abundantly supplied with pure, soft spring water, the *great essentials for hydropathic purposes*.

The bath-rooms have facilities for giving a variety of baths, such as Full, Half, Shallow, Douche, Eye, Ear, Nasal, Spray, Steam, Medicated, etc.

Dr. and Mrs. O. V. THAYER have the entire charge of the Medical Department. Their large experience and extensive public and hospital practice for more than twenty years, and the success attending their labors, gives them confidence in recommending their Institution as a place where sick people *can be cured*. Surgical as well as medical cases are solicited. All needful surgical operations skillfully performed, and the hygienic treatment, so successful to rapid recovery, continued at the Cure when necessary,

They have made diseases of WOMAN their *special* study. Ladies who have been long suffering from any of the diseases peculiar to their sex, will here receive proper and judicious treatment, as well as realize the additional advantage of having a physician of their own sex to whom to make known their wants.

SOLAR RAY SURGERY.—They are also prepared to remove all Surface Affections, such as Moles, Mothers' Marks, Discolorations, Knobs, Fungoid Growths, India Ink Marks, Powder Marks, Cancer Warts, Congenital Nævi, Common Warts, etc., etc., only by the concentrated rays of the Sun, producing not a drop of blood, and leaving no permanent Scar.

Terms from $10 to $16 per week. Surgical operations and extra attention an additional charge. Patients will provide for personal use 3 linen or cotton sheets, 2 woolen blankets, 6 towels, and 2 table napkins, all of which should be marked. Patients are required to pay in advance for the first two weeks, as we take no one for a less period.

For further particulars address

O. V. THAYER, M. D.

In the late nineteenth century many people believed that certain waters had curative effects upon a number of maladies. The natural springs of Mount Prospect became a perfect site for the development of the Binghamton Water Cure. The cure and other similar area cures lasted for more than half a century and were a drawing card for visitors to the community. Courtesy of Broome County Historical Society

In addition to the Binghamton Water Cure, Mount Prospect was also home to a brewery. This engraving from an 1866 Broome County atlas shows the operation of the Binghamton Lager Beer Brewery. Several breweries operated in the area during this period. Most remained in business until the early twentieth century. The Bates Troy cleaners on Laurel Avenue in Binghamton is housed in a former brewery building. Courtesy of Broome County Historical Society

Known by some as "the mysterious mayor," Walton Dwight (1837-1878) was elected to the city's highest position in 1871. He was born in Windsor and served in the Civil War as a colonel. In 1868 Dwight moved to Binghamton and purchased the Orchard, the home of Daniel Dickinson on Front Street. After the home burned, Dwight hired architect Isaac Perry to design the Dwight House (later called the Dwight Block) on his property. Completed in 1873, the hotel was the most elaborate structure in the city at that time. Dwight also completed Dwight Park across the street and the Dwightsville complex of over thirty homes.

Within a few years, however, Dwight was financially ruined, and his name was connected with several "shady" dealings, including the Cardiff Giant scheme perpetuated by Binghamton cigar manufacturer George Hull. His death in 1878 was suspicious, especially after the discovery of several large life insurance accounts taken out shortly before his death. Eventually an inquest ruled his death was due to natural causes, and his wife inherited a large sum of money. Courtesy of Broome County Historical Society

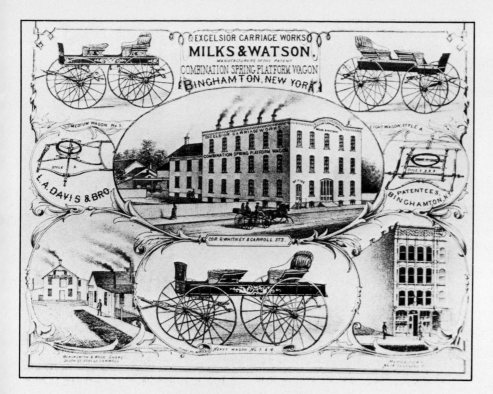

The end of the Civil War brought changes in the nature of the industrial structure of the valley. The prominent raw lumber industry was transformed into a finished goods industry. Wagon and carriage construction was found in several local firms. The best known of these firms were Milks and Watson (depicted here), Crandal, Stone and Company (which opened in 1879 and later became Brewer-Tichener on Upper Court Street) and the Binghamton Wagon Works which operated into the late nineteenth century. Courtesy of Broome County Historical Society

Crandal, Stone and Company employees lined up for a photo. Courtesy of Broome County Historical Society

A rare look at the Dwight Block from Dwight Park on Front Street. Taken in the late 1880s this stereoscopic view shows the last two sections of the eight-sectioned building. The building was converted into a luxury hotel by T. I. Lacey, a protege of Isaac Perry. Dwight spent $80,000 to furnish the hotel's one hundred rooms. The park was completed shortly after the building was opened and included a fountain and a bandstand. As a result of Dwight's financial failure, the park was split into lots in 1882. The Dwight Block was used for apartments and offices until it was demolished in 1982. The bandstand was incorporated as part of a home built on Mac-Donald Avenue. Copied by Marjory Hinman; original owned by Robert Connelly; courtesy of Broome County Historical Society

The men and one boy of the Binghamton Wagon Works. Courtesy of Broome County Historical Society

The history of the local fire departments dates back to 1834, when the village of Binghamton was incorporated. At that time residents had to provide at least two leather buckets to be used in case of fire. Service could be denied if the buckets were not available. When Binghamton became a city in 1867, the movement to create a full-time fire department began. Its present form began in 1888, when a new city charter was incorporated. This lithograph from 1888 shows the winning Alert Company Fire Team, located on Front Street, in a contest held in Philadelphia. Courtesy of Broome County Historical Society

In the mayoral race in Binghamton in 1872 Sherman Phelps was running unopposed. For many voters the candidate was not an ideal choice, and a write-in campaign to elect Old Bay Tom, a former slave, began. Often seen carrying a sandwich board on city streets, Tom ended the election with more votes than Phelps. It appeared that Binghamton had its first black mayor, but the board of electors did not sign the election results and declared Tom ineligible on a technicality. Sherman Phelps received the office, and Tom continued to work odd jobs until his death. His wife, an escaped slave, worked for the Gates family in the town of Maine for many years. Courtesy of Broome County Historical Society

The arrival of the railroad spelled the end for the Chenango Canal. In the 1860s, in an attempt to bring more money, efforts had begun to expand the canal to Owego and connect it to Pennsylvania's waterway system. An extension of the canal through Binghamton was completed by the early 1870s, and the new terminus near Rockbottom Dam would allow it too cross the Sus- quehanna River to connect it with a never-completed canal. This 1870s photograph shows a now-empty canal in downtown Binghamton. The bed of the system was filled in and State Street was created. The unfinished canal system on the south side was used for the Vestal Parkway construction in the 1960s. From the Putnam Collection; courtesy of Broome County Public Library

This photograph from the nineteenth century shows the Spaulding House, a Binghamton hotel which was located near the railroad yards adjacent to Chenango Street. The picture dates from approximately 1870. Courtesy of Broome County Historical Society

An early photograph of the city's fire company taken about 1880 on Hawley Street in back of the third courthouse. The County Clerk's office is seen on the far left of the picture, and the Perry Block appears to the courthouse's right. Courtesy of Binghamton City Historian.

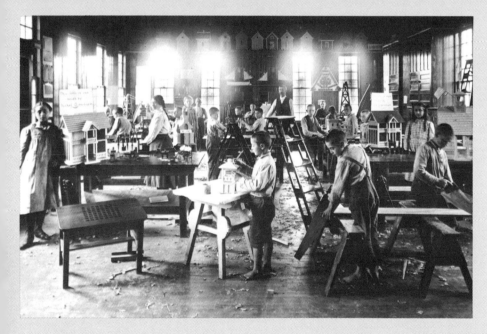

In 1869 the Susquehanna Valley Home was opened on Binghamton's south side. Under the leadership of Dr. John Orton, the home was created in an effort to stop orphans from being placed in the "poor house." The main building, seen in this 1871 photograph, above, housed the children, provided them with education and training, food, clothing, and classes such as the woodshop class depicted in the 1870s photograph, at left. Both boys and girls participated together in these classes. The main building was demolished in the 1950s to be replaced with cottages to provide a more home-like atmosphere for the residents. The home ceased operations in the early 1980s. Courtesy of Broome County Historical Society

On May 18, 1871, a hanging took place on the lawn of the Broome County Courthouse. Edward H. Ruloff was hanged for the murder of Frederick A. Merrick, a store clerk, who Ruloff shot and killed in the course of a robbery. Ruloff, probably one of New York State's first serial killers, was suspected of killing his wife and daughters in Ithaca some years before. He was convicted of kidnapping his wife (the bodies were never found), but won on appeal. He was immediately arrested for the murder of his daughter. He escaped and was linked to several robberies throughout the region for many years. During this

time Ruloff passed himelf off as a professor of languages (he actually wrote a book on the subject).

He was linked with the son of one of his jailers. With a third individual, these men robbed the Halbert Brothers store in Binghamton. After Merrick's death, Ruloff apparently murdered both of his accomplices, whose bodies were found the next day. Ruloff never expressed guilt or remorse, but instead condemned those about to view his hanging. *From* Courier Magazine, *September 1956 courtesy of Broome County Public Library*

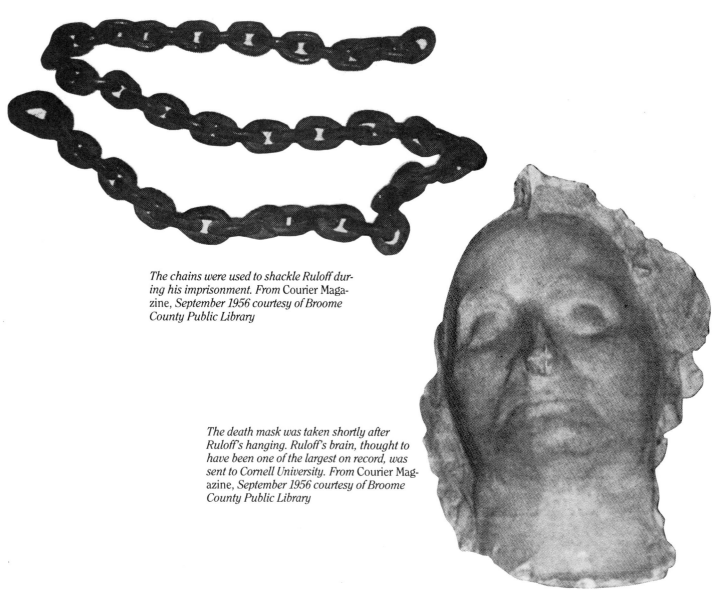

The chains were used to shackle Ruloff during his imprisonment. From Courier Magazine, *September 1956 courtesy of Broome County Public Library*

The death mask was taken shortly after Ruloff's hanging. Ruloff's brain, thought to have been one of the largest on record, was sent to Cornell University. From Courier Magazine, *September 1956 courtesy of Broome County Public Library*

FIRST MEETING
OF THE
BINGHAMTON DRIVING PARK
ASSOCIATION,
AT BINGHAMTON,
Wednesday and Thursday, July 28 and 29, 1869.

$2,100 IN PREMIUMS!
First Day, Wednesday
No. 1.   PURSE $150.
For all Horses that never Trotted for money better than 3 minutes, prior to June 1st, 1869.

$100 to First. $30 to Second. $20 to Third.

No. 2.   PURSE $300.
For all Horses that never Trotted for money better than 2.37, prior to June 1st, 1869.

$200 to First. $70 to Second. $30 to Third.

No. 3.   PURSE $250.
For Double Teams owned in the City of Binghamton, July 1st, 1869.

$150 to First. $75 to Second. $25 to Third.

Second Day, Thursday
No. 4.   PURSE $200.
For all Horses that never Trotted for money better than 2.50, prior to June 1st, 1869.

$125 to First. $50 to Second. $25 to Third.

No. 5.   PURSE $1,200.
OPEN TO THE WORLD.

$800 to First. $250 to Second. $150 to Third.

CONDITIONS.
All the above purses are for mile heats in harness, best three in five, except No. 3, which is for best two in three.

All entries must be made on or before 4 o'clock P. M. July 27th, at the Office of the Treasurer, H. S. JAMES, Binghamton, and an Entrance Fee of 10 per cent. of the purse accompany the entrance. Three to enter and two to start. Any horse entering, and not eligible, will forfeit his entrance.

When a horse has a record of less than the required time, made on ice or on a short track, it will be no bar; if it be proved to the Judges that such record could not have been made on a full track.

All purses will be paid from the Judges' stand as soon as the race shall be decided.

Trotting according to the Rules of Union Course, and to commence each day at 1 1-2 o'clock precisely.

D. S. RICHARDS, Sec'y.   J. S. WELLS, Pres't.

CHARLES VAN BENTHUYSEN & SONS PRINT, ALBANY.

This broadside indicates that interest in horse racing began in the area after the end of the Civil War. Although the race was held under the name of Binghamton Driving Park Association, the actual meet took place in Union. Horse racing would be held in that location, the site of the current Union-Endicott football field, throughout the remainder of the nineteenth century and much of the twentieth. Courtesy of Broome County Historical Society

Despite the creation of the Union Free School System in New York State after the Civil War, private schools continued to operate successfully. This photograph shows Mrs. Duke's School located at 66 Hawley Street. Mrs. Duke had been a student at Miss Barton's school, one of the most successful private schools in the area. Mrs. Duke received her certificate from Missouri in 1872 and operated her own school at various sites throughout Binghamton for over thirty years. The building seen in the photograph still stands. From the Putnam Collection; courtesy of Broome County Public Library

The move to treat indigency began early in the area's history. In 1830 the Broome County Poor House was created. Within a year, land on Front Street, near present-day Broome Community College, was purchased. The Alms House, seen in this photograph, was the complex's main building. Children, insane, and poor were originally housed at the site. Eventually only the sick remained on the complex as the Broome County Infirmary, which at one time included a working farm. The Broome County Home ceased operations in the 1960s. The Alms House has been restored and is used for classes by Broome Community College, located nearby. Courtesy of Broome County Historical Society

By the late nineteenth century many conditions such as alcoholism and mental disease were seen as treatable. In 1858 the New York State Inebriate Asylum was opened on the eastern hill overlooking Binghamton. Begun by Dr. Frederick Turner of New York City, it was the first such institution to treat acloholism as an illness. The asylum eventually ran into financial and managerial difficulties, and in 1879 the state changed the name and emphasis of the institution to the Binghamton Asylum for the Chronic Insane. Architect Isaac Perry was hired to design and build the main building, seen in this 1880s lithograph. The Castle, as it has become known, still stands on the grounds of the Binghamton Psychiatric Center. Courtesy of Broome County Historical Society

The American institution of the five-and-ten-cent store began in the last half of the nineteenth century. This photograph of Walker's "5, 10, and 25 cent store" at 109 Court Street shows the hodgepodge of items which made the Woolworth and Kresge families millions of dollars. It was commonly called "Penny" Walker's. Mr. Walker is standing at the door. From the Putnam Collection; courtesy of Broome County Public Library

This photograph shows the home of the Egbert Gaige family. Located at 10 New Street in Binghamton, the home was distinctive for its oversized brick construction, unusual for this area. In the early 1980s the home was renovated and restored and is today used as an office of the Haskell Associates in Real Estate. From the Putnam Collection; courtesy of Broome County Public Library

The House of Good Shepherd building was founded by Mrs. Helen S. Wright and the Ladies of Christ Church in 1870. It was located on Conklin Avenue and was used as the area's first hospital, the first home for the aged, and the area's first day nursery. Courtesy of Broome County Historical Society

The care for the elderly was bettered in the late-nineteenth century with the opening of several nursing homes in the community. Fairview Home on Binghamton's east side has been this area's longest and most successful such operation. The original residence was opened in the last quarter of the century. Courtesy of Broome County Historical Society

Cigars were hand rolled from the tobacco
until automation sped the process of manufacture in the early twentieth century. Despite
protests from employers, women continue to
roll the tip of the cigar in their mouths to form
the shape of the ends. The holders for
completed cigars can be seen on the work

Chapter Six

"Segars" and the Parlor City 1880 to 1905

For the people of Broome County, the turn of the nineteenth century seemed like the best of times. Newspapers constantly bombarbed the populace with advertisements for new businesses, while more and more products were produced locally.

The groundwork for this expansion could be found in the changes following the Civil War. In the last two decades of the nineteenth century, those changes came to fruition and the area saw unprecedented growth. The most significant factor in this growth was the rise of the manufacture of cigars in the Binghamton area. Although the first cigar factory opened in 1858, it was not until the late 1870s that the industry became the leading employer within the region.

The valley offered the industry a good means of transporting the tobacco into the area, relatively low rents and real estate costs, and an ample supply of cheap labor. The number of factories operating in the area grew continually for the next four decades, until over fifty firms were involved with the manufacture of cigars. Over five thousand people were eventually employed in the industry, many of them women and immigrants. Binghamton became second in the country in the number of cigars manufactured; second only to New York City.

Several other firms also experienced a meteoric rise during this period. The fortunes of the Kilmer family who would wield great power in later years, were amassed from the laboratories and assembly lines of their patent medicine firm, which produced Swamproot Medicine. In the mid-nineteenth century a small boot and shoe manufacturing firm began. The Lester Brothers Boot and Shoe Company continued to grow, especially after the firm's sale to Henry B. Endicott of New England. He hired a young supervisor named George F. Johnson, who would later become his partner, to oversee many of the local operations. Within a few years the company had grown to the point where larger quarters were necessary. Johnson realized that the lands lying to Binghamton's west were ideal for business growth, and the company moved to Lestershire (incorporated as a village in 1892). The Endicott-Johnson Corporation, as the firm would later be called, became one of the area's leading employers.

In 1889 a small firm called Bundy Manufacturing Company began producing a new type of time recording device. With money provided from several investors in the Binghamton and Oneonta areas, the firm marketed their product in this country and abroad. Within a few years they were absorbed into a conglomerate of firms involved in related fields. The company needed larger quarters and moved westward to property owned by the Endicott-Johnson Corporation. By the early years of the twentieth century, this firm, now called International Time Recording Company, was becoming a major force in the area.

Many other types of companies opened in the last years of the 1800s, manufacturing a variety of products: washing machines, metal products, clothing, and furniture. The common thread among all these firms was the need for labor. The necessity for unskilled workers led to the call abroad for immigrants to come to the United States and seek their fortune in the factories of the valley.

They came to the area by the thousands; from the countries of Eastern and Southern Europe and Russia they left their homelands, where poverty, religious persecution, and political strife had taken their toll. In the ten short years between 1870 and 1880 the population of Binghamton more than doubled, from just over seventeen thousand to more than thirty-five thousand residents. Natives of Italy, Germany, Czechoslovakia, Rumania, and the Ukraine, among others found new homes in the neighborhoods of the city. Farmers, as well, tired of the constant battle with the elements, moved into Binghamton hoping to find their own fortunes, while numbers of workers in the coal fields of Pennsylvania came out of the mines to seek new opportunities.

The money that resulted from the manufacture of millions of cigars each month spilled over to the other industries of the area, bringing with it the opportunity to create hospitals, opera houses, and libraries. Thousands of homes were constructed throughout the region during this period. These Victorian homes with their subtle grandeur added to Binghamton's image as The Parlor City, where residents could sit and relax on their front porches and watch a bustling, modern city at work.

To the west of the city lay the lands of Lestershire, Union, Hooper, Vestal, and the new village of Endicott. As the city of Binghamton filled with immigrants, homes, and businesses, these lands held the promise for even further expansion. Already people were moving to the western part of the valley. They followed the rivers, just as the Indian had so many years before. As the twentieth century arrived, the valley was continuing to undergo a transformation.

One of the most successful of the private
academies was the Lady Jane Grey School.
This interior view epitomizes the decorum
established by the school. The school opened
in 1861 in the old Brandywine Hotel built in
1810 by Joshua Whitney at Court and Liberty
streets. It closed in 1923, and the building was
removed in 1926 for the city's gas works.
*Courtesy of Broome County Historical
Society*

This broadside advertised the Susquehanna
Seminary, located on Binghamton's west
side. The private school opened in 1855. By
1881 the school had closed and the building
became St. Mary's Orphan Home. It was
demolished in 1963 to make way for Catholi
Central High (now Seton Catholic High
School). *Courtesy of Broome County Historical Society*

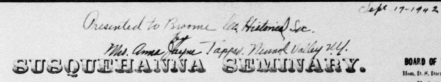

SUSQUEHANNA SEMINARY.

Binghamton, Broome County, New York.

DESIGN AND PLAN.

THIS INSTITUTION is designed to prepare Students, by a liberal, thorough and practical education for college, the study of a profession, the counting-room, or any business of life which literary and scientific acquirements may improve and adorn. The course of instruction is thorough and comprehensive; and the discipline kind but firm, aiming at strict order, prompt obedience, correct deportment, and earnest industry. The plan unites, with the most careful attention to health, improvement in personal habits and manners, faithful religious instruction, and a complete preparatory course in English, the ancient and modern Languages, and the Sciences.

LOCATION.

BINGHAMTON is justly celebrated for the healthfulness of its climate, beauty of its scenery, for the Christian intelligence, and refinement of its inhabitants. Situated on the New York & Erie Railroad, and being the terminus of the Syracuse and the Delaware & Lackawana Railroads, it is easy of access from all parts of the country.

BUILDINGS.

THE SEMINARY BUILDINGS are new and commodious, and being situated on an eminence which overlooks the entire village, they afford a beautiful view of both the Chenango and Susquehanna Valleys, and the surrounding scenery. The Boarding Hall is separate from the Seminary Building, and is under the most excellent and efficient management. The Students rooms are each designed for two occupants, contain a large wardrobe, and are eleven by twenty feet in size. The North Halls are occupied by the Gentlemen, and the South by the Ladies; while, between, in the centre building, are the Chapel, Parlor, and the Teachers rooms. Besides these, the main building contains Recitation Rooms, Library, Society Rooms, Laboratory, Lecture Rooms, &c.

THE GROUNDS (about ten acres,) are much the greater portion of them devoted directly to the recreation of the pupils.

TEACHERS' CLASS.

A Class will be formed in the Spring Term for the accommodation of such as desire to become Teachers, whose tuition is paid by the State.

Students applying for admission to this Class must be—Ladies sixteen, and Gentlemen eighteen years of age; and required to sign a pledge, certifying their intention to teach a reasonable length of time.

EXPENSES.

Board, Washing, Furnished Room and Tuition, in Common English, per year, (in advance.).. $100 00

TUITION FOR A TERM OF 11 WEEKS.

Common English........................ $5 00
Higher English.......................... 7 00
Ancient and Modern Languages........ 8 00
Incidental Expenses..................... 50

EXTRAS.

Lessons on Piano....................... $10 00
Use of Piano............................ 2 00
Oil Painting............................. 10 00
Perspective Drawing.................... 5 00
Vocal Music (two Lessons a week.)..... 2 00

☞ All Tuition to be paid in advance.

BOARD.

Board, including washing, and furnished rooms, $2.25 per week. $2 will be charged in the Winter Term for fuel, and $1 in the Spring and Fall Terms. Rooms are supplied with bed, table, three chairs, wash-stand, and box for fuel. Students take care of their rooms, and are expected to furnish their lights, wash-bowls, pitcher, mirrors, towels, brooms, pails, and one comfortable, each.

☞ Board bills are to be paid, one-half at the commencement and the other half at the middle of the Term. No deduction made for brief absence, nor for leaving before the close of the Term, except in cases of illness.

TERMS AND VACATIONS.

1860 { First Term opens August 15th.
First Term closes October 26th.
Vacation twelve days.
Second Term commences November 7.

1861 { Second Term closes March 7th.
Vacation nineteen days.
Third Term opens March 26th.
Third Term closes July 1st.
Vacation six weeks.

☞ The opportunities afforded for improvement in Debate are of a high character. A Literary Society, holding weekly meetings, is in a flourishing condition, and occupy rooms set apart for this purpose.

GRADUATING COURSE.

FIRST YEAR.

English Grammar........................Clark.
Geography, (Ancient and Modern,)
........................Finley & McNally.
Arithmetic............................Davies.
Physiology...........................Cutters.
History, (Ancient and Modern,)......Wilson.
Book-Keeping.......................Payson & Co.
Natural Philosophy....................Wells.
Algebra, (commenced.)................Davies.
French...............................Fasquelle.
Latin.......................Richard's Lessons.
Grammar..........Andrew & Stoddard.
Reader........................Andrews.
Greek..........................Crosby's Lessons.

SECOND YEAR.

Rhetoric..........................Quackenbos.
Algebra, (continued.)................Davies.
Geometry............................Davies.
Chemistry............................Wells.
Astronomy...........................Burritt.
Intellectual Philosophy..............Upham.
French......Fasquelle, Telemaque, Corinne, and French Testament.
German......(optional.) Woodbury's Course.
Latin......Caesar, Virgil, Arnold's Prose Composition.
Greek.....................Anabasis, (Owens.)
Greek Testament.

THIRD YEAR.

Trigonometry..........................Davies.
Mensuration and Surveying............Davies.
Analytical Geometry..................Loomis.
Botany...............................Gray's.
Logic................................Whately.
Elements of Criticism................Kames.
Evidences of Christianity.............Paley.
Moral Philosophy.....................Wayland.
French.................Robertson & Racine.
Latin......Cicero Orations, Livy and Horace, (Lincoln's.)
Greek..................Homer's Iliad, (Owen's.)

☞ Diplomas awarded to Graduates.

French optional with Gentlemen.

Ladies may substitute an equivalent in Ornamental Branches for Ancient Languages and Higher Mathematics.

Declamations and Compositions weekly.

Lectures, with illustrations and experiments, will be given each Term in Philosophy, Chemistry and Astronomy.

There is no Primary Department connected with the Seminary.

Elementary Classes in Grammar, Arithmetic, and Geography will not be formed, except when essential deficiency in Students shall require it.

BY-LAWS.

1. Students will arise in the morning at the ringing of the bell.

2. Students will not throw anything from their windows, nor will they sweep dirt into the halls, except on Saturday.

3. Students may not leave their rooms during study hours, except for recitations.

4. Students will be responsible for injuries done to their rooms or to the furniture.

5. Students will not leave the premises without permission.

6. Students may not use gunpowder about the buildings.

7. All games of chance are strictly forbidden.

8. Students are required to abstain entirely from the use of intoxicating liquors while members of the Seminary, and not to smoke on the premises.

9. Students will repair to their rooms promptly at the ringing of half past 9 o'clock bell, and remain there for the night.

10. Students may not congregate in the halls, or be guilty of boisterous conduct either in the halls or rooms.

11. All Students attend religious service on the Sabbath, at the place designated by their parents or guardians. When no designation is made, then Students and Teachers attend together.

12. Ladies and Gentlemen are permitted to associate only in the presence of Teachers, except on the common play ground between the Seminary and Boarding Hall.

13. Damage done to furniture or rooms, will be assessed to those occupying them.

14. Any Student who shows a disposition to evade the above Rules, and persist in so doing, will be sent home.

N. B.— By prohibition in the Insurance Policy, Students are not permitted to use Camphene or Burning Fluid.

REV. E. OWEN, AGENT.

The area has had its own "police constable" since 1834, but it was not until 1881 that the first police commission was created for Binghamton. This early photograph was taken during a parade of city departments. Courtesy of Broome County Historical Society

The Binghamton Fire Department on parade and two of its stations, located on Water Street, at top, and De Russey Street at bottom, (now the Number 5 restaurant) as they appeared at the beginning of this century. Courtesy of Broome County Historical Society

This building is believed to have been the first water works building on Court Street near the Brandywine Creek and constructed about 1867. The water works complex was used into the twentieth century. Courtesy of Broome County Historical Society

To honor the Broome County men who gave their lives during the Civil War, this monument was erected on the courthouse lawn in 1888. This picture from Binghamton Illustrated *(1890) shows Fireman's Hall on Collier Street in the rear of the photograph. Courtesy of Broome County Historical Society*

Between Water Street and the Chenango River a complex of structures arose to operate the city's first gas works business. This photograph was taken about 1885. The gas works would later move to Upper Court Street opposite the Tompkins Street bridge. Courtesy of Broome County Historical Society

As Binghamton grew so did the need for better transportation. Trolleys drawn by horse had been used for several years when the electric streetcar was introduced to the city in 1886. It was the first electric car in New York State. Trolleys were replaced by buses in 1932. Courtesy of Broome County Historical Society

The home of Waring Weed on the southeast corner of Chenango and Henry streets in Binghamton was constructed in the 1850s. In 1920 the Morning Sun *building incorporated the home as the core of its new headquarters. From the Putnam Collection; courtesy of Broome County Public Library*

A long line of voters waited for their turn to vote at Fireman's Hall in front of the home of Dr. Titus Brown on Collier Street. The home was originally constructed by his father-in-law, Brazilla Marvin. The building was demolished in 1896 for the construction of a new City Hall (now the Hotel DeVille). Courtesy of Broome County Historical Society

The Columbian bicycle was manufactured in Binghamton during the mid-1880s. Here Robert Dekin of Lowville, New York, is shown with one of the firm's products. Photograph by John Warner; courtesy of Binghamton City Historian

In 1865 the two Noyes brothers began a small comb factory in Binghamton. Within a few years the business moved to a mill property near Water and Lewis streets. For over sixty years the company continued to produce combs and buttons in Binghamton. The factory abutted the Chenango River, and an island which was adjacent to the complex of buildings was connected to the eastern bank of the river in the twentieth century. Many residents still refer to this area, which includes Piersons Office Supply Center, as Noyes' Island. Courtesy of Broome County Historical Society

The furniture business flourished in the valley in the last half of the nineteenth century. Firms constructed large factories next to railroads to allow both raw materials and finished goods to be transported. The Binghamton Chair Company was one of the more prominent of these firms. Located on Montgomery Street in Binghamton, the building today houses Pa's Woodshed and the world's largest chair. Courtesy of Broome County Historical Society

During the Civil War, Nelson Stow discovered the principle of transmitting power at an angle at his buggy whip shop in Center Village, New York. A few years later he began the manufacture of flexible shafts in Port Dickinson. The business grew rapidly, and, as this broadside indicates, moved to larger quarters in Binghamton. Although product lines have altered through the years, the company continues to operate and prosper in facilities which once housed the Link Company on Binghamton's east side. Courtesy of Broome County Historical Society

As the population grew, so did the need for better medical facilities. In 1888 the first City Hospital opened in the Lowell Harding house on Court Street. The hospital operated on this site until 1895, when it moved to the present south side location. *Courtesy of Broome County Historical Society*

For many years the south side of the city was connected to the downtown by this pedestrian bridge located at the end of Exchange Street, now the site of the Exchange Street bridge. Broome County's third courthouse can be seen in the rear of the photograph. *From the Putnam Collection; courtesy of Broome County Public Library*

A rare "bird's eye" photograph of the city of Binghamton taken somewhere between 1883 and 1886. The foreground shows the largely undeveloped south side of the city with the unused portion of the Chenango Canal that would later become the bed of the Vestal Parkway. The covered bridge over the Sus-quehanna River appears without its roof and side boards, which were removed to lighten the weight of the bridge after its condition deteriorated. In the area adjacent to the bridge can be seen the Weed Tannery complex, which eventually employed over one hundred workers. To the left of the plant is a small octagonal building which was part of the "old" gas works. The area's third courthouse appears in the center of the picture, with the Phelps bank building on the corner of Court and Chenango streets. From the Putnam Collection; courtesy of Broome County Public Library

The Washington Street bridge was erected over the Susquehanna River in 1886. It replaced the covered bridge that occupied that site. Constructed of iron and designed by William Douglas of Binghamton, the structure is one of the last triple parabolic arch bridges left in New York. Although it closed in the 1970s, it now awaits reconditioning and reopening to traffic. Photograph by John Warner; courtesy of Binghamton City Historian

Cigars were the leading product of Binghamton during the last quarter of the nineteenth century and the first quarter of the twentieth. The Westcott Building, housing the firm of H. Westcott and Son, was one of fifty factories operating during this time. Located on State Street, the original structure (shown here) was built in 1882, and as the business expanded, the later stone-front building was used in many capacities, including the Riley Business School, until its demolition for redevelopment. The George A. Kent factory was on Chenango Street, while Barlow, Rogers, and Simpson was located on Wall Street. Both of these buildings were torn down in the 1960s for urban renewal. The new Sheraton Hotel, built in 1987, today occupies the Barlow factory site. Courtesy of Broome County Historical Society

The Westcott stone-front building. Courtesy of Broome County Historical Society

The George A. Kent factory. Courtesy of
Broome County Historical Society

Barlow, Rogers, and Simpson. Courtesy of
Broome County Historical Society

This artist's rendering shows the home of Hull, Grummond and Company located at the corner of Henry and Water streets in Binghamton. A major manufacturing factory of cigars in the city, the structure today is occupied by Cahill Office Center. Courtesy of Broome County Historical Society

As the cigar industry blossomed in Binghamton, so did the need for more employees. Immigrants, especially female immigrants, were welcomed as employees of most factories. This photograph shows the Cigar Manufacturing Department of the F. B. Richards Cigar and Company. Courtesy of Broome County Historical Society

Labor unrest tugged at the structure of the local cigar industry during much of its operation. Several strikes, especially one in 1890, hurt the productivity of the business. Both males and females walked strike lines and several labor unions thrived during this period. As seen in this photograph of the F. R. Richards Cigar Factory, women and children were a significant part of the work force. Women eventually made up two-fifths of the total number of workers. Courtesy of Broome County Historical Society

Beginning in 1854, the Binghamton Iron Works produced metal castings, heating apparatus, and heavy iron goods at its plant at the corner of Hawley and State streets. The name later changed to Shapley and Wells and continued in operation into the early twentieth century. Courtesy of Broome County Historical Society

This photograph dating from 1885 shows Dr. Doan's Sanitorium, which was located on Glendale Drive in the town of Union. It occupied a site near the present IBM Glendale Laboratory. From the collection of the George F. Johnson Memorial Library; courtesy of Lawrence Bothwell

In 1878 Binghamton became home to Dr. Kilmer and Company, a patent medicine firm that blossomed with the manufacture of Swamp Root medicine. For the next six decades the firm prospered under the leadership of Jonas Kilmer (1844-1912), who bought out the firm from his brother, S. Andral Kilmer. Courtesy of Broome County Historical Society

This advertising card from the 1890s shows the laboratory and factory of Kilmer and Company in the upper left corner. The plant was located on Chenango Street near Stow Flats until a fire largely destroyed the struc- ture. A new factory and modern laboratory was constructed on the corner of Chenango and Lewis streets. The building now houses the Lander Company. Courtesy of Gerald R. Smith

When the major power of Dr. Kilmer and Company was given to Willis Sharpe Kilmer (1868-1940) by his father, Jonas, he used his business acumen to build on that base and create a large empire of wealth and influence. He took several millions of dollars out of the company to create the Binghamton Press Company, after a rival newspaper had printed an unflattering story about him. With success in these two ventures, Kilmer built an estate on Riverside Drive which included a one million dollar stable complex to raise and train thoroughbred horses. Sun Briar Court was the home of Exterminator, who won the Kentucky Derby in 1917. Today Willis Kilmer's home is Temple Israel, and the clubhouse of the stables is used by Lourdes Hospital. Courtesy of Broome County Historical Society

The interior of the Kilmer laboratory on the corner of Lewis and Chenango streets. As was typical of the period, women did much of the assembly line work such as in the boxing department, while men were employed in the clerical and manual labor areas as seen in the packing department shown at bottom. Courtesy of Broome County Historical Society

Cures for ailments were not limited to the patent medicines and the spring waters of Mount Prospect. S. Andral Kilmer (of Swamp Root fame) had a sanitarium at Sanitaria Springs and a cancertorium in Conklin. The area also saw the development of genuine medical treatment with the opening in 1905 of the Tuberculosis Hospital also known as Mountain Sanitarium near the State Hospital. The hospital closed and reopened in 1919 near the Chenango Bridge area. It expanded many times, eventually becoming the Chenango Bridge Nursing Home. Courtesy of Broome County Historical Society

In 1889 Harlow Bundy began the Bundy Time Recorder Company, manufacturing a device invented by his brother, W. L. Bundy. Although the firm began with little money, Bundy was able to attract funds from several investors, and soon the time recorder was marketed in areas throughout the world. This photograph shows the firm's headquarters on Water Street, shortly before the company left Binghamton. The business merged with other related firms and became the International Time Recording and Tabulating Company. The firm moved to the new village of Endicott in 1905. In the 1920s, under the leadership of Thomas J. Watson, the firm would change its name to International Business Machines—IBM. Courtesy of Broome County Historical Society

Isaac Perry was one of New York's foremost architects during the nineteenth century. He was appointed state capitol architect, and designed the "million dollar staircase" in that building. Locally, Perry designed the main building at the Binghamton Psychiatric Center, the Monday Afternoon Club home, several churches, the Dwight Block, and this building, known as the Perry Block. His office and apartment were on the top floor of the bulding, the only cast-iron structure left in the city. For many years it was home to Hills, McLeans, and Haskins Department Store, and is now the new home of the downtown branch of the Endicott Trust Company ("The hometown personable bank"), one of the sponsors of this book. From Binghamton Illustrated (1890); courtesy of Broome County Historical Society

Retail trades increased with the rise of industry in the Binghamton area. Hills, McLeans, and Haskins was one of the area's first department stores. This photograph, taken by E. E. Conrad of Olean, shows the store's employees. Department stores opened up the employment of women as store clerks, a position often previously held in smaller stores by men. Courtesy of Broome County Historical Society

Located at 154 Washington Street behind the City National Bank, the J. E. Searles and Son Confectionary Shop operated during the 1980s. The shop, which also sold fruit and other food items, was typical of the small "mom and pop" operations which proliferated well into the twentieth century. Courtesy of Broome County Historical Society

The construction of a fairgrounds in Binghamton led to an annual fair being held there until it relocated to Whitney Point in the early twentieth century. The fairground was located on Stow Flats, near the present-day Binghamton Plaza. This photograph shows the main area of the grounds, which opened in 1892. From the Putnam Collection; courtesy of Broome County Public Library

The American pastime, baseball, invaded Binghamton in the last quarter of the nineteenth century. In 1892 a local minor league team called the Bingos were champions in their league. The team continued to play in the area for many years, but would move to the Lestershire area in the early twentieth century. After that area became Johnson City, the team would change its name to the Triple Cities. The name would be shortened to the Triplets. *Courtesy of Broome County Historical Society*

A man's home is his castle, or so it seems in this view of homes along Main Street in Binghamton in 1890. From Binghamton Illustrated *(1890); courtesy of Binghamton City Historian*

In 1875 Erastmus Ross donated ninety acres on the south side of Binghamton to the city for a public park. The Common Council accepted the offer and renamed the site Ross Park in August of that year. This view of the park in the 1890s does not show the zoo area. Thought to have been the second oldest zoo in the country (it ranks among the first ten zoos), the zoo continues to operate, now under the leadership of the Southern Tier Zoological Society. The park was connected to the city by the trolley system and provided a carousel for children (donated by George F. Johnson). Donated by Elizabeth Letson; courtesy of Broome County Historical Society

In 1854 Elijah Brigham located in the town of Union in the area that would become Johnson City. He operated a brickyard near his home on Main Street for many years. When his original frame structure became too small, he built a large brick home that would later become Your Home Library. Courtesy of Broome County Historical Society

By the last quarter of the century, railroads had an impact on an area much larger than Binghamton. The new means of transportation brought businesses, goods, and people to the western portions of Broome County. The new village of Lestershire was growing rapidly. This 1890 photograph shows the first depot (for the Delaware, Lackawanna, and Western Railroad) built in the village. A hotel is to the station's left, and the Pioneer Factory of the Lester Brothers Boot and Shoe Company is in the rear. Courtesy of Your Home Library

Charles Quick opened his drugstore on Main Street in Lestershire in 1898. Although the business moved across the street after this picture was taken, it is still in operation today. Mrs. Quick and her daughter are seen in front of the store. Courtesy of Broome County Historical Society

HOAG BLOCK   Grant Chambers   Mrs. F.M.Duryea   F.M.Duryea   J.F.Chambers

Kennedy Block   Clayton   Lestershire N.Y.   Spring 1890

The Hoag Block in Lestershire as it appeared in the spring of 1890. The building housed many occupants, including Mr. and Mrs. F. M. Duryea, Clayton Duryea and Grant and J. F. Chambers. The site was later used for the construction of the Kennedy Block. Courtesy of Your Home Library

This building was constructed in 1897 in a block-wide area of Lestershire for the Faatz Brush and Felting Works. In later years the firm was commonly called the Felters Company and operated well into the twentieth century. After the company ceased operations the building became the home of the Lescron Book Outlet Company, which used it as its headquarters until that firm closed in 1986. Courtesy of Broome County Historical Society

Education spread throughout the area during the latter portion of the nineteenth century. Public schools were constructed to house the ever-increasing numbers of students. This photograph shows the old Stella schoolhouse near present-day Johnson City. Stella was a small settlement named for the daughter of one of the early residents. The route of the Stella Ireland Road passed through this hamlet to an area of Irish inhabitants known as New Ireland. From the Putnam Collection; courtesy of Broome County Public Library

The Imperial Hotel in Lestershire as it appeared in the summer of 1903. Frank Griffin was listed as the hotel's proprietor. The building later became the Grand View hotel on Willow Street. Courtesy of Your Home Library

Lestershire's Henry B. Endicott fire station and team was located at the corner of Corliss Avenue and Willow Street in 1899. The fire station would later be replaced by the new municipal building. Courtesy of Broome County Historical Society

An early view of Ackley Avenue in Lestershire at the turn of the century. The corner lot on the right side of the picture would later be used for the Primitive Methodist Church. Courtesy of Broome County Historical Society

See TITLE on the Other Side. **Souvenir of Lester-Shire, N.Y.** E. K. STURDEVANT, Photographer.

Entitled "A Birds-Eye View of Lestershire, North," this photograph dates from about 1891. The First Baptist Church on Baldwin Street can be seen in the center. Courtesy of Your Home Library

The lumber business had been a prevalent part of the area's economy since white settlers arrived in the 1700s. The need for lumber continued in the later 1800s with furniture and carriage manufacture. Alonzo Roberson and his son operated a major lumber business until the 1940s. This photograph shows his lumber yards at 313-345 Chenango Street in Binghamton. From the Putnam Collection; courtesy of Broome County Public Library

The westward movement of industry began in the later 1800s, and Alonzo Roberson saw the chance to strengthen his lumber business. He moved to land which transversed the line between Binghamton and Lestershire (John-son City). The new lands were cheaper and tax rates were lower than the city, and seemed an ideal location for the growth of the manu-facturing section of the area's economy. Cour-tesy of Broome County Historical Society

The employees of the Sturdevant-Larrabee Company about 1900. The firm, which produced carriages and sleighs, was located on Charles Street in Binghamton's First Ward. From the Putnam Collection; courtesy of Broome County Public Library

Taken in 1899, this photograph shows the workers of the Wilkinson Manufacturing Company in Binghamton. The firm produced furniture for many years. An interesting note on late-nineteenth century fashion is that everyone in the photograph is wearing a hat. From the Putnam Collection; courtesy of Broome County Public Library

"1900" WASHER CO.

CATARACT MACHINES
8 and 12 Sheet Capacity

All Metal Machine, Swing Reversible Wringer, No Cylinder to Lift Out and Clean. The Machine with the Perfect Figure 8 Motion, Forces the Water In, Under, Over and Through the Clothes.

The home of S. Mills Ely, which was located at 85 Henry Street in Binghamton. Ely was a wholesale grocer and furniture manufacturer whose philanthropic efforts included the Humane Society, the Fresh Air Movement, and the donation of his summer home on Mount Prospect to be used as a city park. Today's residents still enjoy the park and golf course that Binghamton maintains at Ely Park. From the Putnam Collection; courtesy of Broome County Public Library

"We are such stuff as dreams are made on" wrote Shakespeare, and the Commercial Travelers Home was the valley's dream. It was intended to be a massive estate on Binghamton's South Mountain to be used as a haven for traveling salesmen. The groundbreaking ceremonies were accompanied by a large parade and the publication of an elaborate program written in the shape of a steamer trunk. Like many dreams, this one vanished with most of the money intended for construction. The remains of the outline of the building were covered after years of abandonment. The cornerstone was moved to the old City Hall and now resides at Roberson Center. From the Putnam Collection; courtesy of Broome County Public Library

Constructed around 1870 and designed by Isaac Perry, the Sherman Phelps mansion on Court Street in Binghamton represented the home of the elite. In 1890 the house was sold to the Monday Afternoon Club, which still operates from this site. The mansard roof was removed in this century. From Binghamton Illustrated; *courtesy of Binghamton City Historian*

A familiar building to many residents of the Triple Cities, this 1879 brick structure was constructed to house Binghamton's Union Free Schools numbers 2 and 3, and was located at the corner of Washington and Hawley streets. It would be home to the Union Free School Library, the predecessor of the Binghamton Public Library. After 1914 it became police headquarters. It was razed in 1969 for the Marine Midland Plaza building. Courtesy of Broome County Historical Society

Court Street was bustling in 1890. This view shows the Great Fair store on the right. The store would move across the street and operate for nearly a century. Above the Fair Store are the offices of E. E. Vosbury, architect of Alonzo Roberson's home on Front Street (now Roberson Center). From Binghamton Illustrated; courtesy of Binghamton City Historian

1898

THE NEW CENTRAL OFFICE AT

177 STATE STREET

MISS KATHERINE C. FAHEY,

NOW MRS. WILLIAM R. ELY,

CHIEF OPERATOR IN CHARGE.

MR. W. CLAYTON SEXSMITH

APPOINTED MANAGER.

BINGHAMTON'S POPULATION

39,647

The first owner of a telephone in Broome County was Joseph Noyes of the Noyes Comb Factory (1880). This photograph was taken around 1900 in the offices of the New York and Pennsylvania Telephone and Telegraph Company. It would later merge with Bell Telephone and relocate to Henry Street in 1912. Courtesy of Broome County Historical Society

The entrance to Bennett Park about 1900. The park was located on Binghamton's west side and opened on lands originally called Bennett's Grove in the late 1890s. The land gradually developed into housing with the exception of a large area donated to the city by George F. Johnson to be used as a public park called Recreation Park. From the Putnam Collection; courtesy of Broome County Public Library

Binghamton grew at an incredible pace in the last years of the nineteenth century. New buildings went up faster than ever before. Here a construction crew works on Henry Street around 1885. The Hotel Bennet can be seen on the right-hand side of the photograph. Courtesy of Binghamton City Historian

As the number of students grew in the late 1800s, so did the need for larger school buildings. Although the old Binghamton Academy on Courthouse Square was used as a high school for several years, by 1870 a new high school was under construction on Main Street in Binghamton. Designed by Isaac Perry, the building was completed in 1871. Seen in this postcard, the school would be removed in 1913 to build the current high school. Courtesy of Binghamton City Historian

The rivers have always been a source of fun, power, and water for the area. This 1890 view of the Susquehanna shows the Castle of the Inebriate Asylum, later Binghamton Psychiatric Center, on the upper left. The smokestack of the city's water works can be seen in the middle of the photograph. From Binghamton Illustrated; courtesy of Binghamton City Historian

The Athletic Club House in Binghamton was located on the south side of the Susquehanna River. It served as a place of enjoyment well into the twentieth century. From Binghamton Illustrated; courtesy of Binghamton City Historian

On December 28, 1896, the county's third courthouse, to which two additions had recently been made, caught fire. In a desperate effort to save the structure the city's fire department struggled against the rising flames amid the cold of a winter's night. Spectators tried to help by carrying furniture, books and records out of the back of the building. The fight was fruitless, and the building collapsed in ruins, leaving only a portion of the walls as a reminder of the graceful structure. This painting of the conflagration is by C. M. French and now hangs in the lobby area of the Binghamton City Hall. Photograph by Marjory Hinman; courtesy of Broome County Historical Society

The first post office in the area opened in 1795, but in 1891 a new facility began operations on Wall Street in Binghamton. The structure served as both the post office and federal government offices. The building was scorched by the flames of the Binghamton Clothing Company fire in 1913. A new post office opened in 1934 on Henry Street, and the old building was demolished in 1942. At the time of its demolition, the building, which was supposed to have been of solid stone construction, was found to have had a stone facade covering a mainly wooden frame. *From* Binghamton Illustrated; *courtesy of Binghamton City Historian*

Gustav Stickley manufactured furniture in Binghamton for a few years prior to his move to Chicago. Another brother continued the operation here under the name of the Stickley-Brandt Company. This 1890 photograph shows the Stickley Brothers Furniture store near the corner of Henry and Washington streets. *From* Binghamton Illustrated; *courtesy of Binghamton City Historian*

The shape of Endicott had only begun to form when this photograph of the new village was taken in 1901. The first Endicott-Johnson complex in Endicott had started construction. The Dusenburg farm can be seen in the lower right of the picture. From the collection of the George F. Johnson Memorial Library; courtesy of Lawrence Bothwell

The Hotel Frederick was built by the Endicott-Johnson Corporation to house visitors to the new village of Endicott then under construction. It was located on the corner of Washington Avenue and Main Street. It opened on April 1, 1906. From the collection of George F. Johnson Memorial Library; courtesy of Lawrence Bothwell

Graced by Victorian interior decoration at its highest, the studio of L. J. Buckley was located in the Morning Sun *building at Henry and Chenango streets. From the Putnam Collection; courtesy of Broome County Public Library*

On May 20, 1903, the Rockbottom Bridge over the Susquehanna River collapsed while a trolley car was crossing. This dramatic photograph from the Binghamton Herald newspaper shows the rescue attempts at freeing the passengers and the conductor, who was injured when he was thrown from the car into the river during the accident. He was able to swim back, though, and aid two female passengers. From the Putnam Collection; courtesy of Broome County Public Library

A view of Lestershire near the intersection of Corliss Avenue and Baldwin Street, taken in 1903. Courtesy of Your Home Library

This water tower was constructed next to the Floral Park Cemetery in Johnson City. The gravestones can be seen in the foreground of this 1903 photograph. Courtesy of Broome County Historical Society

A new building was needed to handle Lestershire's government staff. The 1904 photograph shows the Municipal Building on Willow Street. The structure housed the village offices, the fire department, and the police department. Courtesy of Your Home Library

A view of Main Street in Lestershire looking west from Willow Street as it appeared in approximately 1904. Courtesy of Your Home Library

The home of Orlow Chapman on Exchange Street and Congdon Place. Chapman was a Binghamton attorney of some note in the last quarter of the nineteenth century. The house was demolished in 1903 to make way for the Binghamton Public Library. From the Putnam Collection; courtesy of Broome County Public Library

On October 15, 1903, William Phelps lowered a time capsule into the cornerstone of the future Binghamton Public Library. The library was the gift of Andrew Carnegie, who gave the city seventy-five thousand dollars towards the construction of the building. The city purchased the Orlow Chapman home as the site of the new building, and promised to continue to support the library by giving at least $7,500 for an annual budget. The building housed an auditorium and museum on its second floor and opened with a staff of four. The library has been the Broome County Public Library since 1985 and has a staff of over forty, five branch libraries, and an annual budget of over one million dollars. Courtesy of Broome County Public Library

The Broome County Public Library. Courtesy of Binghamton City Historian

The Hagaman Block appears in this photograph on the corner of Court and Exchange streets in Binghamton. The Pope building is on the right of the Hagaman Block. Both buildings were constructed in 1870. The picture dates from 1904, shortly before both buildings were demolished to make way for the Security Mutual Building. The Binghamton Public Library, then under construction, can be seen on the far right. From the Putnam Collection; courtesy of Broome County Public Library

Designed by T. I. Lacey, the Press Building on Chenango Street began construction in 1904. Seen in this architect's sketch of the proposed structure, the building was for many years the tallest building in the Triple Cities. Indeed, Willis Kilmer insisted that additional floors be added to ensure it be taller than the Security Mutual Building constructed at the same time. It is interesting to note that the building in the lower right-hand corner of the sketch closely resembles the Binghamton Public Library, which S.O. and H. A. Lacey were constructing nearby. Courtesy of Broome County Historical Society

Workers on the Court Street bridge, near the trolley tracks. The trolley system connected Binghamton with Johnson City and Endicott, allowing the population to move easily from place to place. The spires of the Isaac Perry-

Chapter Seven

Creation of the Triple Cities
1905 to 1920

In 1906 the village of Endicott was formally incorporated, creating the final link in what became known as the Triple Cities. The three municipalities of Binghamton, Lestershire (which would be renamed Johnson City in 1916), and Endicott shared a common transportation system, industrial base, and heritage. During the two decades after Endicott's incorporation the area saw ever-increasing numbers of immigrants arriving. The phrase "Which way E-J?" (for Endicott-Johnson) became synonymous with the new residents.

Agriculture continued to play an important role in the areas surrounding the Triple Cities, providing residents of the urban areas with food. The farming community took the lead in organizing itself and created the nation's first Farm Bureau, located in the Town of Chenango in 1911.

In 1914 Thomas J. Watson came to the village of Endicott as the new president of International Time Recording Company. Within a few years he led the company away from possible stagnation and into new areas of development and productivity. His one-word philosophy, "Think," became as recognizable as did the new name for the firm, International Business Machines—IBM.

George F. Johnson continued to expand the Endicott-Johnson Corporation, purchasing tanneries and processing plants in other parts of the northeastern United States that could aid with the production of shoes. George F. promoted his "square deal" philosophy after wondering "if it would not be better to give more attention to the human side—that workers had hearts as well as hands, and that a leader of industry shouldered certain responsibilities beyond pocketing the profits." He soon realized that the success of his business lay not with the numbers on a ledger, but that "results are measured by the health, happiness, satisfaction and thrift of the people who are making the business...for if these relations are favorable better boots and shoes are sure to follow." Johnson began a long family tradition of philanthropic efforts: donating pairs of shoes to each schoolchild; giving hospitals, libraries, and parks to the communities; and helping thousands of workers build inexpensive homes.

In 1916 the Endicott-Johnson company took the lead locally by lowering the number of hours required to work from nine and one-half hours to eight. The parade to celebrate this event demonstrated the genuine feeling that those workers had for their employer. In other areas, however, working relationships were not as pleasant. The cigar industry had undergone several major strikes by labor unions organized to protect the worker from the sometimes unscrupulous wage cutting techniques of the employer. These constant labor upheavals only served to weaken the industry, and the numbers of workers employed in the field began to drop. The introduction of automated machinery further reduced the work force, and the popularity of the cigarette cut deep into the cigar industry. By the early 1920s only the smaller, handmade cigar-making "factories" were in existence.

The working conditions of the workers were seriously questioned after the Binghamton Clothing Company building on Wall Street caught fire in July 1913. In a few horrible minutes the entire four-story brick structure went up in flames with over one hundred people in the building. As the smoke cleared, the smoldering ruins revealed that thirty-two persons had died in the conflagration (all but two were women). The mass burial in Springforest Cemetery of the twenty-one unrecognizable bodies was attended by hundreds of residents.

On the national scene, Woodrow Wilson had made a campaign promise to keep "your sons out of war." But the strain of alliances and world politics proved to be too strong and the nation was plunged into what many called "the war to end all wars." Hundreds of young men from the area volunteered to fight for their nation, and others were called up to continue the fight during 1917 and 1918. Many veterans returned disillusioned with society, hoping to create a better order that could prevent such utter destruction. Others never returned at all, having been buried on the battlefields of Europe.

As the end of the second decade of the century approached, the workers of the Endicott-Johnson company collaborated to create a monument to George F. Johnson and his philosphy. A fitting selection was made, and monies were contributed by the employees of the company. In 1920 construction of two arches was completed, one at the entrance of Johnson City and the other at the border of Endicott, announcing to the world that this was the home of the "square deal." It was also a symbol of the healing of war wounds and the passing of mourning; the future lay just ahead.

In 1905 a tornado hit the area, causing major damage to a number of houses in the region. The south side of Binghamton was the scene of the largest devastation, as seen in this photograph of the destroyed B. L. Smith home on Kress Street. From the Putnam Collection; courtesy of Broome County Public Library

Ely Tower was constructed by S. Mills Ely as part of the park on Mount Prospect which he gave to the city in 1907. The tower collapsed during a strong windstorm and was removed. Today the site is part of the municipal golf course. From the Putnam Collection; courtesy of Broome County Public Library

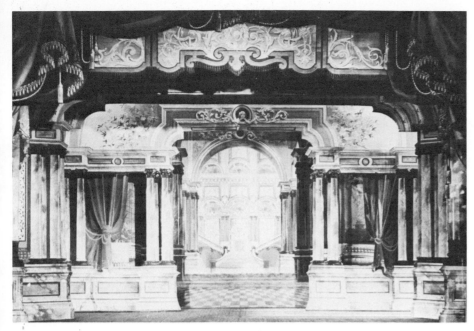

The interior of the Stone Opera House. The building, constructed in 1892 on Chenango Street, was the scene of hundreds of operettas, lectures, and vaudeville shows. It was soon converted to show "moving picture shows" as well as live performances. In recent years it became the Riviera Theater and is now undergoing renovation. From the Putnam Collection; courtesy of Broome County Public Library

Movie houses began springing up across the country at the turn of the century. The Empire Theatre was located at 101 Court Street in Binghamton, and in this 1907 photograph, the triple-feature included A Military Prison and Sold By Arabs. The cost was five cents. The site now is occupied by the Broome County Travel Agency. From the Putnam Collection; courtesy of Broome County Public Library

By the 1920s the rise in popularity of the cigarette and the automation of the manufacture of cigars had seriously hurt the local cigar industry. This postcard advertisement is from Hummell and Company on Lewis Street. Courtesy of Broome County Historical Society

Home of TOM PLATT Five Cent Cigar
HUMMELL & CO.
Manufacturers,   Binghamton, N. Y.

When rainy is the weather,
    And dismal all things are,
I pull myself together
    And light a "Platt" cigar.

And with the wreathes of
        smoke, sir,
    My spirit comes to par,
Misfortune's but a joke, sir,
    If I've a "Platt" cigar.

And whether fortune makes
        me
    A super or a star,
I'll have it--if it breaks me--
    A Tom Platt cigar.

The band for this cigar, named in honor of George F. Johnson, is from the Thomas Thorne Company. Courtesy of Broome County Historical Society

GEO. F. JOHNSON

REGISTERED
Manuf'd by Thos. Thorne, Binghamton, N. Y.

The entrance to Wagener's Park in Johnson City on Riverside Drive. The park opened in 1902 and soon became a popular amusement park. The site (also called White City) was sold in 1910 for use as Bible School Park, later to change its name to Practical Bible Training School. Few of the original buildings remain at the school today. Courtesy of Broome County Historical Society

WAGENER'S PARK

The offices of the Morning Sun *prior to 1920. The newspaper, through various names, dated back to the 1930s. In the 1960s it merged with the* Evening Press *under the ownership of the Gannett Corporation and today is the* Press and Sun-Bulletin. *Courtesy of Broome County Historical Society*

The railroad industry brought ont only business, but also a need for passenger stations. The Lackawanna Station was built at the turn of the century and continued to serve passengers until the mid-1960s. It has now been rehabilitated and offers elegant space for offices and stores. Courtesy of Broome County Historical Society

The Fairbanks Valve Company opened its doors in Binghamton in 1909, although the history of the company dates to the mid-nineteenth century in New England. The firm manufactured valves, scales, trucks, pulleys, and a number of other products. The pattern shop, seen in this photograph, would later become the administrative offices for the firm. As the company evolved, so did the type of products turned out by the local plant. The company was closed in 1985, and the plant on Binghamton's west side was demolished for the development of a shopping plaza. Courtesy of Broome County Historical Society

The trolley system was well established by the first part of the twentieth century, allowing residents to go from Ross Park in Binghamton all the way to Casino Park in the town of Union (Endicott). Here trolley car number 301, which ran on the Endicott and Union line, is shown. Courtesy of Broome County Historical Society

Nothing is certain except death and taxes, but especially death. One of the more elaborate hearses of the area is seen in this photograph in front of Kent's Cigar factory in Binghamton in the early years of the 1900s. Courtesy of Broome County Historical Society

The Vestal schoolhouse. It was torn down in 1952 just as Vestal was poised for its great expansion in population and business growth. Courtesy of Broome County Historical Society

Although major businesses did not appear in Vestal until after World War II, there were a number of small companies that provided a variety of products and services. Seen in this photograph is the creamery that was located at Vestal Center. Another firm in the area was Stafford and Lee, which manufactured shirt collars and cuffs. *Courtesy of Broome County Historical Society*

The Marshall Furniture Factory began production in Lestershire in the late part of the nineteenth century, an example of the westward movement of industry from Binghamton. *Courtesy of Your Home Library*

134

Within a few years after the first Lester Brothers shoe factory was built, the village of Johnson City entered an incredible period of growth. This view of the area shows the spread of residences southward from the downtown area to Floral Avenue near Willow Street. From the Clarence Livingston photograph collection; courtesy of Your Home Library

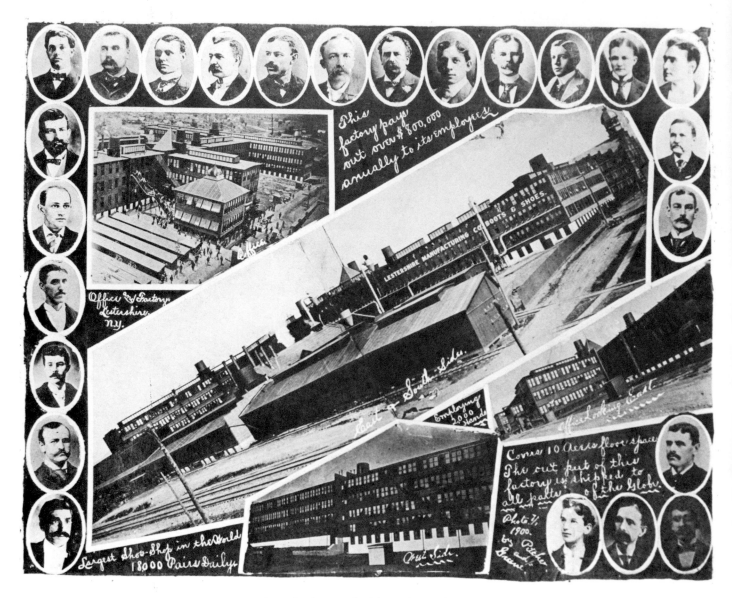

An early photograph of the Endicott-Johnson factory complex in Lestershire. Although the first factory, the Pioneer Factory, was not as large, the buildings covered over ten acres at this time. In 1916 the village was renamed Johnson City in honor of the company's president. Courtesy of Broome County Historical Society

The unique shape of the familiar building belongs to the Powell Coal Company on Clinton Street in Binghamton. The building could hold ten thousand tons of coal at one time, and continues to be used for storage and recycling purposes. *From* The Valley of Opportunity; *courtesy of Binghamton City Historian*

Designed by S. O. and H. A. Lacey, the Boston Store opened on the corner of Court and Water streets in 1899. The store later changed its name to Fowler, Dick and Walker, and this 1920 advertisement indicates that it was the area's largest department store for ninety years. It was closed in 1981 and reopened in 1984 as Boscov's department store. *From* The Valley of Opportunity; *courtesy of Binghamton City Historian*

WHERE
EVERYBODY
STOPS
AND
SHOPS

OVER
THREE ACRES
OF
FLOOR
SPACE

"50 SPECIALTY STORES IN ONE"

Some of Our Feature Attractions:

THE MILLINERY SALON
Largest and finest in the Southern Tier.

WOMEN'S APPAREL SECTION
Where Quality and Moderate Price meet.

THE BASEMENT SALESROOM
The lower-price "Store Within a Store."

THE MEN'S CLOTHES SHOP
Ready-to-wear Clothing and Custom Tailoring.

THE TEA ROOM
Daily club luncheon and a la carte service.

THE MUSIC ROOM
Pianos and Phonographs, world-renowned makes.

FREE PARCEL-CHECKING SERVICE
MAIN FLOOR

REST AND WRITING ROOMS
THIRD FLOOR

FOWLER, DICK & WALKER
Binghamton's Representative Department Store

The Lestershire Band in front of the village's municipal building in 1910. Music was an important cultural feature in the Triple Cities, and each area had its own local band that would perform in the town's bandstand. Courtesy of Broome County Historical Society

Agriculture had been a part of the area since before white men ventured into the region. Local farms provided the residents of the valley with food and dairy products for years. As the population moved from the city and spread further into the farm lands of the area, farmers began to retreat from the area. Some farmers would give up that business in the hopes of finding a better life on the assembly lines of local industries, while others moved further west and northward, away from the developing urban area. This photograph of the author's grandfather, William J. Smith, dates from about 1915. Courtesy of Robert W. Smith

Local aviation history dates back to the days of the Wright Brothers. This photograph shows the airplane of James J. Ward, one of those daring young men in their flying machines, after he had landed it on Stow Flats in Binghamton on September 28, 1911. Courtesy of Broome County Historical Society

Main Street in Johnson City developed largely between 1890 and 1920 and remarkably retains much of its original character today. Courtesy of Your Home Library

Many residents of Johnson City enjoyed the pleasures of swimming in the old "brick pond," which was located near the present-day George F. Pavilion at CFJ Park. The pool was heated by discharge water from a steam plant. It was later replaced by the huge above-ground pool in the park. From the Hilla Hatch Kinney photograph collection; courtesy of Your Home Library

In 1915 Casey Day was celebrated to honor Daniel Casey of Binghamton. Casey, a baseball player in the latter part of the nineteenth century, claimed to have been the inspiration for the "Casey At The Bat" poem. He later returned to the area and worked as a streetcar conductor. He is seen here in the center of the back seat of the automobile, seated next to George F. Johnson (on Casey's right). Courtesy of Broome County Historical Society

George F. Jo[...] (1857-1948) came to this area in h[...]g twenties from Massachusetts to work for the Lester Brothers Boot and Shoe Company. When Henry B. Endicott took control of the business, Johnson was made superintendent. In 1899 he was made a partner and later ran t[...]ire operation. The Endicott-Johnson Company would employ 18,000 workers and "George F." and his "industrial democracy" would influence the area's entire economy. This photograph was taken about 1923 to be used as a model for the statue of Johnson which is located in Recreation Park in Binghamton. The girl who modeled for the statue is local resident Dorothy Joggerst. Courtesy of Broome County Historical Society

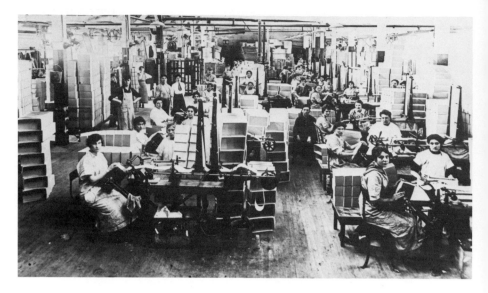

Diversity in industry continued into the twentieth century with the development of book printing. The Vail-Ballou Company was incorporated in 1910, absorbing the old Binghamton Book Manufacturing Company and, after 1913, moving to Jarvis Street. Workers in the plant are seen in this early photograph. Today the company continues to manufacture a number of paper-and-book-related products. Courtesy of Broome County Historical Society

The Phelps Bank Building graced the corner of Court and Chenango streets from 1871 to 1929. Designed by Isaac Perry, it housed a bank on the street level and a number of offices. It was replaced by the First National Bank, now Chase Lincoln First Bank. From the Lester Lee Cole collection; courtesy of Broome County Historical Society

Fire in the Thompson Store and Cobb's Photo Gallery on Court Street brought out hundreds of downtown residents in November 1913. The store's site is now occupied by MetroCenter. The familiar shape of the Press Building can be seen through the smoke. From the Putnam Collection; courtesy of Broome County Public Library

The home of the telephone company from 1915 to 1931 at 62 Henry Street. The building was replaced with New York Telephone's current structure. Courteys of Broome County Historical Society

One of the area's major department stores, Sisson Brothers and Weldon Company was in business for over a century on Court Street. This photograph was taken during World War I. Courtesy of Broome County Historical Society

In 1917 Your Home Library opened in Johnson City, a gift to the community from George F. Johnson. It opened in the Brigham homestead on Main Street. The building also housed classes, lectures, groups and even dinners in its large meeting rooms on the second floor. Today the library has five times the original number of books and is the Johnson City center for the Susquehanna Urban Cultural Park. From the collection of Your Home Library; photograph by David Dunda; courtesy of Lawrence Bothwell

The tensions of European politics proved too strong to avoid, and the United States became a part of the First World War in 1917. Thousands of men from the Broome County area volunteered to fight in the war effort or were drafted into the service of their country. This photograph shows one of the various ceremonies for the local soldiers which were held before they left for Europe. Courtesy of Broome County Public Library

St. Paul's Episcopal Church was constructed on the corner of Broad Street and Jefferson Avenue on land donated by George F. Johnson. Dedicated in 1911, the church was a further step in the organization of the new village of Endicott. From the Putnam Collection; courtesy of Broome County Public Library

The Children's Home of the Wyoming Conference was organized in 1919 by the Methodist Church to provide a home and center for needy children. The main structure seen in this photograph was dedicated in 1922. The facility continues to serve children from throughout the area. Courtesy of Broome County Historical Society

The Sturdevant-Larrabee Company began manufacturing wagons in Binghamton in the late nineteenth century. The company was successful in this effort, but within a few years the change in technology to motorized vehicles forced an attempted adaption to the manufacture of trucks. From the Lester Lee Cole Collection, courtesy of Broome County Historical Society

778

The Sturdevant-Larrabee Company went
through a period of adjustment, restructuring
itself as the Larrabee-Deyo firm, producing
trucks, such as this one, well into the 1920s.
Courtesy of Broome County Historical
Society

"What a revoltin' development this is" might
be the caption for this picture. By the 1920s
the old wooden sidewalks that had graced the
city of Binghamton for many years had worn
out and the need for newer, more modern
concrete sidewalks was apparent, especially
in this rather staged photograph. Courtesy of
Binghamton City Historian

Cutler Ice Company on Front Street in Binghamton appears in a photograph from 1920. The firm processed ice formed on Cutler Pond near present-day Elizabeth Church Manor and sold it to homes and businesses throughout the area. Today the Magic City Ice Company still manufactures ice from the same building but without use of the pond. From The Valley of Opportunity; courtesy of Binghamton City Historian

The second home of the hospital in Endicott. It was located on Main Street across the street from the first hospital. The home was used for medical care from 1916 to 1927, when Ideal Hospital opened. It was the residence of the Dr. Roger Mead family until 1981. From the Putnam Collection; courtesy of Broome County Public Library

One of the many gifts to the community from the Endicott-Johnson Corporation was Ideal Park in Endicott. Constructed on the land of Casino Park, the park could be reached by trolley or car, and contained the Casino building (seen in the photograph), which was built about 1894 and burned down in 1948, and a race track as well as a large swimming pool, tennis courts, Ideal Pavilion, and Ideal Clubhouse. The park's name was later changed to En-Joie Park. It was closed and removed in the 1960s with the expansion of Route 17, the Southern Tier Expressway. From the Putnam Collection; courtesy of Broome County Public Library

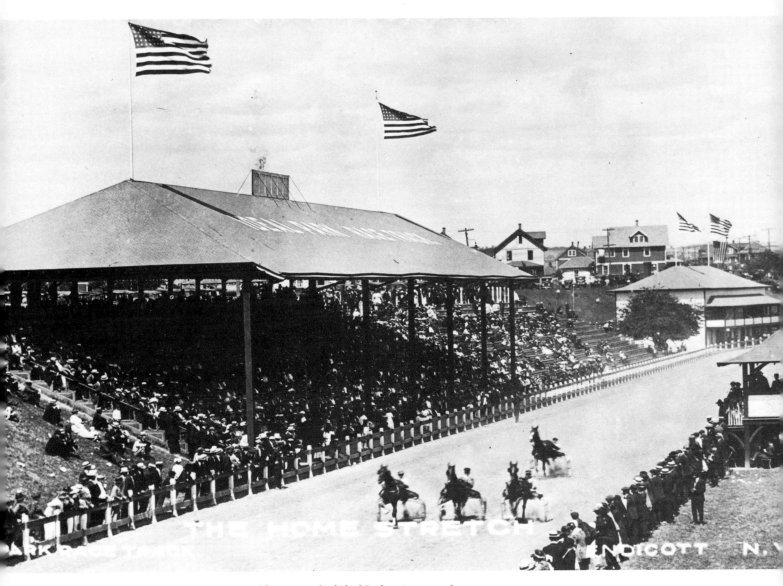

The race track of Ideal Park as it appeared about 1930. From the Putnam Collection; courtesy of Broome County Public Library

The strength of E-J's helped other businesses in the Johnson City area. The Fair Play Caramels Company has been a staple of the area since the 1920s. It continues to operate in its plant on Grant Avenue. Courtesy of Broome County Historical Society

A household name in the Triple Cities in the first half of this century, the Cream Dove company in Binghamton produced a variety of food products, including peanut butter—the type that had to be stirred before it could be eaten. From The Valley of Opportunity; *courtesy of Binghamton City Historian*

For more than half a century Spaulding Bakeries produced baked goods for thousands of area residents. This photograph of the bakery on Exchange Street in Binghamton dates from 1920. The memory of the aroma near that plant still lingers in the minds of many local citizens. Courtesy of Broome County Historical Society

The hubbub of a modern city around the intersection of Court and Washington streets. The City National Bank, which proudly shows paying interest of four percent, was later replaced with the bank building that is today Tiffany's Bank Cafe. From the Putnam Collection; courtesy of Broome County Public Library

The automobile soon became an integral part of the American family's lifestyle, allowing great freedom of movement for all members of the nation. In an early photograph is Charles Quick (driving first car) of Quick's Pharmacy in Johnson City returning home from a World Series game. Courtesy of Broome County Historical Society

The home of George F. Johnson on the corner of Park Street and Lincoln Avenue in Endicott in a picture taken about 1908. The Harlow Bundy home can be seen in the rear of the scene. Courtesy of Broome County Historical Society

"The Lab" building on North Street in Endicott was one of the early buildings in the complex of structures that evolved from Bundy Time Recording Company into IBM. The front of the building's frieze is emblazoned with that company's slogan, "Think." Courtesy of Broome County Historical Society

As the Endicott-Johnson Corporation grew westward, helping to create the village of Endicott, the fledgling IBM settled in the new village to gain a foothold in the industrial world. Within three decades the IBM Corporation had assumed a major role in the community's industrial structure. Courtesy of Broome County Historical Society

The Corbett Mansion on Riverside Drive in Binghamton as it appeared in 1917. In 1925 the house became the first home of Lourdes Hospital, affiliated with the Roman Catholic Church.

An addition was built at a later date, but in 1954 the house was demolished for further growth of the hospital. Courtesy of Broome County Historical Society

The present courthouse as it appeared in the 1920s. Constructed in 1897 after the third courthouse burned, it was designed by Isaac Perry and built by Miles Leonard. The second Universalist Church at Congdon Place and

Exchange Street, currently the site of the Binghamton Savings Bank, can be seen on the far left of the photograph, next to the Binghamton Public Library. Courtesy of Broome County Public Library

An architect's sketch illustrates the Lourdes Hospital after its expansion. It continues to operate as an independent hospital today. Courtesy of Broome County Historical Society

In the first three decades of the twentieth century, thousands of immigrants from Eastern and Southern Europe and Russia fled their homelands for opportunities in the United States. Many came to t█ █ley. The businesses of the area needed cheap labor, which the immigrants provided. The cultural heritage of those groups added a vital element to the ethnic makeup of the community. Many immigrants chose to become citizens of their adopted country in ceremonies such as this one held in the 1950s. Cour█ █
Broome County Historical Society

Chapter Eight

Partners All
1920 to 1941

The large percentage of immigrants in the area led to the rise of organizations that were created to help them adjust to their new environment. The Americanization League began in Binghamton in the early 1920s and held English language and home economic classes for immigrants as well as provided services which helped with the paperwork to bring relatives to this country.

Not everyone in the area felt compassion for the immigrant. At the same time that the Americanization League was operating, the Ku Klux Klan rose to new heights of power. The resurrection of the Klan was felt in the valley. Binghamton became the center for many Klan activities, including a state-wide convention and the intrusion of the group into a mayoral election during the 1920s.

The largest economic factor of the period was the Great Depression. The crash of the stock market in 1929 and the following decade of economic upheaval and dissolution was felt throughout the country. This area was no exception to business failure or families losing their farms because of financial difficulties. In Binghamton and other sites were soup kitchens and meal lines at community houses, but the effects of the Depression was not as severe as in other parts of the nation. The strength of the Endicott-Johnson Corporation, IBM, and Ansco helped to stave off the worst of the economic failure. The companies reduced the hours of many employees, but in doing so were able to minimize massive layoffs.

In the midst of economic disaster in the country, a new firm began in Binghamton which would have a profound effect on the fledgling aviation industry. Edwin Link, a maker of pianos and organs in his father's firm, developed the idea for a trainer for pilots of airplanes in 1928. A year later he began his own business to produce this product and revolutionized the aerospace industry.

As the valley entered the decade of the 1930s the business environment seemed better. IBM was reevaluating its product line, and the local plants began the manufacture of typewriters in 1933. The federal aid programs of the Roosevelt administration helped produce a new post office, a state park, and roads and sewers throughout the area. New technology brought radio to the area in 1927 (with WNBF as the first local station) and buses to replace the streetcars in 1932.

As the world seemed to be righting itself, the community was turned upside down by two floods, in 1935 and 1936. The floods, which caused several million dollars' worth of damage to property and left eighteen persons dead, resulted in a call for adequate protection from flood waters and the creation of the reservoir at Whitney Point.

In Europe the rise of Adolf Hitler wrought both fear and change in the structure of the continent's political system. His invasion of Poland, Austria, and other countries could not go unanswered. The alliance of this country with Great Britain and France brought the United States to the edge of total commitment. As the people of the valley entered the 1940s they faced the real possibility of war. This possibility became reality on December 7, 1941, when the Japanese government ordered the raid on the United States Naval Station at Pearl Harbor in Hawaii. Once again valley inhabitants were sent to fight on foreign soil.

As a prelude to the Roaring Twenties, the Endicott-Johnson Corporation, which was firmly established as the area's leading employer, lowered working hours from nine and a half to eight per day. The company had developed significantly since the opening of its Pioneer Factory in Johnson City, and the cut in hours in 1916 resulted in an employee parade showing their appreciation. Courtesy of Broome County Historical Society

The home of C. Fred Johnson on Main Street in Johnson City. Built near the turn of the century, it became the headquarters for the Johnson City YMCA after Johnson's death. It continues to operate from that site today with plans to expand into new quarters within a short time. Courtesy of Broome County Historical Society

A sanitation crew is ready for work on the west side of Binghamton in this 1920 photograph. Courtesy of Binghamton City Historian

Thomas J. Watson (1874-1956) arrived in this area in 1914 as the new head of the Computing Tabulating Recording Company. Within ten years the name of the firm had changed to IBM, and Watson's business philosophies of company unity and loyalty advanced the firm into the forefront of America's industrial structure. This photograph from the 1950s shows Watson, on the right, receiving an award from Forbes magazine, which acknowledged him as one of the nation's top businessmen. Courtesy of Broome County Historical Society

William Hill of Johnson City began his long public career as postmaster of Lestershire in 1896. He soon became president of the village and was editor and owner of the Lestershire Record by the age of 22. "Billy" Hill served for many years as state senator and congressman, and as advisor to governors such as Thomas E. Dewey, earning him the nickname of Mr. Republican. Courtesy of Broome County Historical Society

Binghamton High School students were photographed playing football on the Stow Flats fairgrounds during the 1920s. Many school sport activities were held at the old fairgrounds before the North High School field was constructed in the 1930s. Courtesy of Broome County Historical Society

The Phelps mansion on Front Street in Binghamton was an elegant Greek Revival estate during the nineteenth century. It was demolished in the 1950s to make way for the Botnick Chevrolet company. Courtesy of Broome County Historical Society

Goudey Station on Johnson City's west side was one of the area's pioneer power stations. It has brought power to the western Triple Cities for many years. Courtesy of Broome County Historical Society

A parade down Court Street followed the dedication ceremonies of the Memorial Bridge, honoring local dead from World War I on Decoration Day in 1925. The kiosk for news announcements, a familar site in front of the Broome County Courthouse, can be seen on the lower left. Construction of a pedestrian safety zone for streetcar boarding appears on Court Street. From the Putnam Collection; courtesy of Broome County Public Library

As Endicott-Johnson expanded during the 1920s it added more structures outside of Johnson City and Endicott to its list of factories. Tanneries were included in the firm's operations to make the production of shoes more efficient. In Binghamton the company purchased the old Weed's Tannery had opened in the mid-nineteenth century and eventually employed over one hundred people. When E-J's bought the plant it changed the name to the B.B.B. Factory. The Endicott-Johnson company also purchased the former Chenango Silk-Factory, pictured below on Robinson Street to be used as a warehouse. Both the warehouse and the old Weed's Tannery were taken down in the 1950s and 1960s for commercial development. Courtesy of Broome County Historical Society

A ghostly image of a trolley car appears in this photograph of the O'Neill Building on the corner of Court and State streets. The building housed Drazen's store for many years, and, although the facade has been altered, it is still in use today. From the Putnam Collection; courtesy of Broome County Public Library

The reflecting pool in Recreation Park, which was donated to Binghamton by George F. Johnson in the 1920s. Within a few years he also contributed the toboggan slide that appears on the left of the photograph. Photograph by John Warner; courtesy of Binghamton City Historian

The Arlington Hotel was built in 1887 on the corner of Chenango and Lewis streets. Several additions were made to the hotel's structure, which was demolished in 1967 for urban renewal. The hotel can be seen on the left side of the photograph. The Hotel Carlton appears in the middle of the block, followed by the First Baptist Church. From the Putnam Collection; courtesy of Broome County Public Library

Fraternal organizations have been a part of the area for nearly two centuries. As the population and businesses expanded westward, these fraternal bodies also followed. The home of the Order of the Sons of Italy on Odell Avenue in Endicott is seen in this 1920s view. From the Putnam Collection; courtesy of Broome County Public Library

An early view of St. Peter and Paul Russian Orthodox Church on Hill Avenue in Endicott. It was the first orthodox church in the area whose congregation consisted largely of immigrants from Eastern Europe and Russia. The land for the church was donated by George F. Johnson. The church was demolished in 1960 to make way for the congregation's present structure. From the Putnam Collection; courtesy of Broome County Public Library

A view of the American House in 1923 on Clinton Street in Binghamton's First Ward. The building was home to branches of the Boys and Girls Club and the Binghamton Public Library. Many operations of the Americanization League, including citizenship and English classes, were headquartered in this building. With waves of immigrants arriving in the area daily during the early years of this century, the American House represented an important link between the new residents and the established local culture. From the Putnam Collection; courtesy of Broome County Public Library

An intriguing feature of the valley has been the concentration of the "gold dome" churches throughout the community. Many are located in Binghamton's First Ward or in the adjoining area of Johnson City, such as St. John's Ukrainian Orthodox Church. This region had the largest concentration of recently arrived immigrants, most of whom worked either for the cigar factories of Binghamton or the assembly lines of the Endicott-Johnson Corporation. Courtesy of Broome County Historical Society

In the years following the end of the First World War a strong nativist sentiment arose throughout the country, sparking a return of the Ku Klux Klan. The group preyed upon the fears of the citizens and promoted hatred against the immigrant, black and Jewish sections of the population. In the decade of the 1920s Binghamton became the center of the Klan's activities in New York State. The Klan held its statewide convention in the area in 1924 and participated in a Binghamton mayoral election. Residents still recall the burning of crosses on Mount Prospect. Their reign was short-lived and by the end of the decade they had lost whatever hold they had had on the community. This photograph was taken at a convention held in nearby Ithaca in the late 1920s. Courtesy of Broome County Historical Society

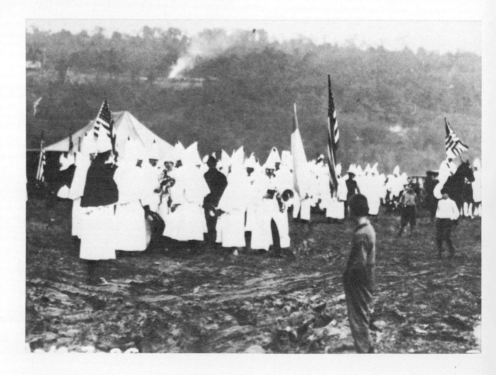

AN E-J. WORKERS
FIRST LESSON
-IN THE-
SQUARE DEAL

George F. Johnson's philosophy of the "square deal" infiltrated all aspects of community life during the 1920s and 1930s. This cover from a pamphlet given to new workers at Endicott-Johnson shows one of the two arches erected in 1920 by workers in the company to honor the Triple Cities, the lifestyle of the area, and George F. Johnson. From the Putnam Collection; courtesy of Broome County Public Library

The Frank M. Smith School building on Harrison Street in Johnson City. It served as a school during the last part of the nineteenth century. As the Charles S. Wilson Hospital expanded, the need for instruction of nurses grew, and the old school became the Nurses Education Building. It was used for this purpose through the 1960s. Courtesy of Your Home Library

One of the related industries that owed its existence to Endicott-Johnson was the Vulcan Corporation located on Grand Avenue in Johnson City. The firm produced shoe lasts and wooden heels. Although that company is no longer operating in the area, the structure is used as the Johnson City location of Philadelphia Sales. Courtesy of Broome County Historical Society

"Come On In, The Water's Fine" was the motto that greeted thousands of bathers for over fifty years. The above-ground pool in CFJ Park in Johnson City could hold two thousand people at one time. It was designed by Wesley Binty in 1927, and was a gift to the community from the Johnson family. The egg-shaped pool was one of the largest in the country and a familiar site to local residents. During the 1960s and 1970s it fell into disrepair, and, despite a valiant effort to preserve it, was demolished in 1982. The George F. Pavilion can be seen on the far left, and the CFJ Park carousel appears in the upper center of the photograph. From the Bob Garvin collection; courtesy of Broome County Historical Society

During the decades of the 1930s and 1940s hundreds of people could hear the strains of Benny Goodman's orchestra playing "Let's Dance" or perhaps Glenn Miller's "String of Pearls" in the pavilion at CFJ Park in Johnson City. The George F. Pavilion provided the opportunity for big bands to come to the valley to play for its residents. The pavilion, a gift of the Johnson family, would be called the Fountains Pavilion after it was purchased by a local restaurant. It is still in use today. Courtesy of Broome County Historical Society

In 1927 this was the home of the Pierce-Arrow Motor Company, but the octagonal building at 23 Washington Street in Binghamton was once used as the tank for the local gas company. Seen in the photograph are Clarence Townsend, on the left, and John Donley, on the right. From the Putnam Collection; courtesy of Broome County Public Library

169

On October 24, 1929, Black Thursday at the stock market, the bottom fell out of the economy. The Great Depression sank the country into an abyss which seemed to have no end; banks failed, businesses closed, people lost their homes, and unemployment reached thirty percent before any relief efforts could alleviate the situation. Locally, however, the depression was not as bleak as in other regions of the nation. The strength of Endicott Johnson, IBM, and several other firms helped to stave off the worst of the

Depression. But no one company could stop all of the effects of the economic crash, and there was still a sizable segment of people unemployed or hungry. The Community Service House (on the left) on Collier Street was the site of one of the local soup kitchens and breadlines. It served the local area by also providing a girls and boys club for a time. In this photograph, the streets adjacent to the building were being paved with bricks. Courtesy of Broome County Historical Society

The New Deal programs of Franklin Roosevelt's administration were seen in the valley during the Depression. The Chenango Valley State Park, the federal post office on Henry Street, the post office in Johnson City, the murals for those buildings, roads, and sewers, such as this one at North Jackson Avenue in Endicott, were all projects of the WPA, the CCC, and the CWA. Courtesy of Broome County Historical Society

In 1928 Edwin A. Link took time away from his father's piano and organ manufacturing business to pursue his interests in the new aeronautical industry. He created a simulator device to aid in the training of pilots. A year later he began his own company which grew steadily despite the Great Depression. The Link Company produced thousands of flight simulators in its early plant near Brandywine Creek (now the home of Stow Manufacturing) and more modern training devices for earth and space travel designed from company headquarters in the Kirkwood Industrial Park. *Courtesy of Broome County Historical Society*

Aerial view of the Link plant near Brandywine Creek. From the Bob Garvin collection; courtesy of Broome County Historical Society

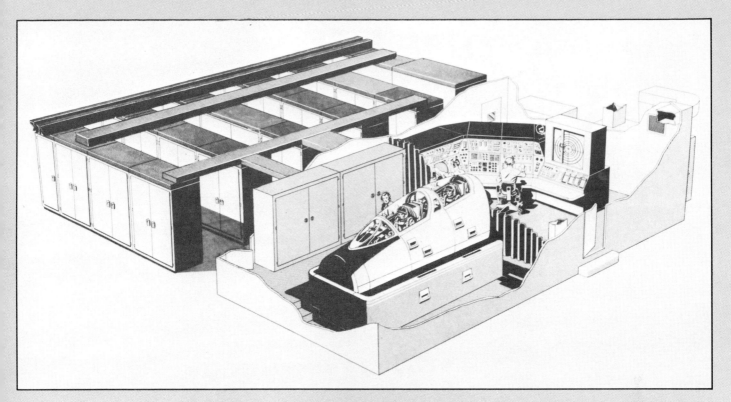

Link training devices at the Kirkwood Industrial Park plant. Courtesy of Broome County Historical Society

The railroad continued to play an important role in the economy of the area throughout the twentieth century, shipping finished goods such as cigars and shoes to worldwide markets. The sight of an engine taking on coal and water such as this one was common during the 1920s and 1930s. From the Lester Lee Cole collection; courtesy of Broome County Historical Society

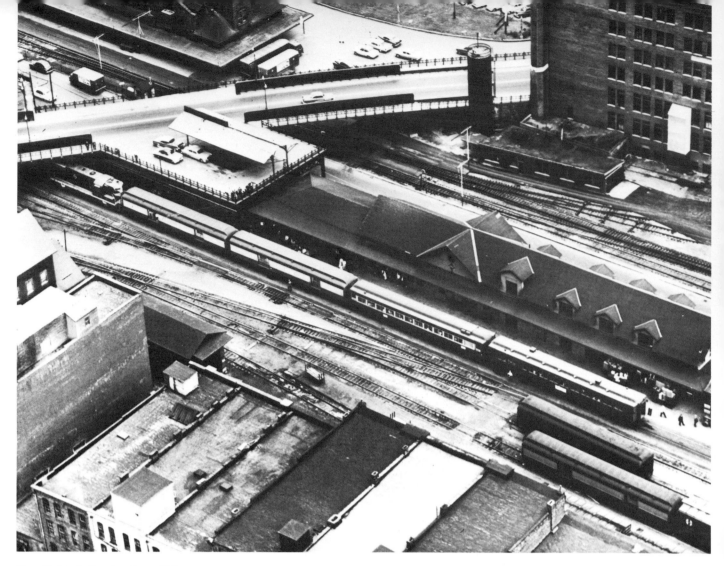

The old Erie Railroad station which once adjoined the Chenango Street viaduct. The Kilmer laboratory can be seen in the upper right of the picture, and the present-day Lackawanna Station appears in the upper left-hand corner. The Erie station was torn down in the 1960s. From the Bob Garvin collection; courtesy of Broome County Historical Society

Medical care improved throughout the period with the expansion of the City Hospital (later renamed Binghamton General Hospital), the creation of the Charles S. Wilson Hospital in Johnson City, and the birth of Ideal Hospital in Endicott. The latter two hospitals were financially supported by the Endicott-Johnson Corporation. This aerial photograph of General Hospital shows the growth in size from the original buildings on the right of the complex. The three hospitals would combine forces under the umbrella organization of United Health Services in the 1970s. From the Bob Garvin collection; courtesy of Broome County Historical Society

Ideal Hospital was closed in the early 1980s and is currently under development as a long-term care facility. The remaining two facilities have undergone a combination and reshaping of their medical care abilities. From the Bob Garvin collection; courtesy of Broome County Historical Society

The agricultural business has been a part of the valley's economy since settlers first arrived. Milk production was the focus of Crowley Foods. The Binghamton firm began in the 1930s with the construction of its south side plant. The firm, now owned by a Dutch company, continues to produce a variety of dairy products for New York State residents. In this early photograph, employees inspect samples of their product. Courtesy of Broome County Historical Society

In 1854 two men named Anthony and Scovill began a small photograph equipment business in Binghamton. The company continued to operate under a variety of names until the establishment of Ansco in the early twentieth century. The firm was consolidated with a German venture into Agfa-Ansco. During World War II the company was seized and operated by the federal government until the 1960s. By then, the firm, known as GAF (General Aniline Film), was a major employer in the area. In the late 1970s GAF sold its photographic division, and the local business was split into two new firms, Ozalid and Anitec. *Courtesy of Broome County Historical Society*

Carl Bormann, an early leader of the Ansco company, is seen with one of the cameras produced at the Binghamton plant near Charles Street. *From* The Valley of Opportunity *; courtesy of Binghamton City Historian*

While flight in the Southern Tier of New York occurred early in aviation history, with pilots such as Carl Rogers, Wiley Post, and Charles Lindbergh landing at local sites, it was not until the 1920s that the first airport was constructed. Bennett Field developed along the Chenango River near present-day Otsiningo Park. It operated until the new Broome County Airport was completed on Mount Ettrick in the mid-1950s. This photograph shows bombers from the Army Air Corps at Bennett Field in July 1933. Courtesy of Broome County Historical Society

During the early morning hours of Monday, July 8, 1935, torrential downpours caused severe flooding in the central New York area. Waters swept away homes, businesses, and lives. Eighteen persons died and $1.6 million in damage was caused by the flood. Bennett Airport and the DeForest Street bridge were impassable, while the Ferry Street bridge (the site of the present-day Clinton Street bridge) which was nearly covered by the waters (shown at top right), collapsed suddenly under the strain of the spreading waters, at bottom right. Newspaper clipping courtesy of Binghamton City Historian. Flood photographs courtesy of Broome County Public Library

THE WEATHER
Cloudy, probably occasional rain today
and Thursday. Colder tonight.

BINGHAMTON PRESS

City Edition

Vol. 57, No. 288.   THIRTY PAGES   WEDNESDAY EVENING, MARCH 18, 1936   PRICE THREE CENTS

WATERWORKS SHUTDOWN, 6 BRIDGES CLOSED, RIVERS HIGHEST IN HISTORY

U. S. Flood Control Action Demanded at Once

Families Fleeing Homes; Workers Build Barricades

City Has Only 24-Hour Supply of Water—No Relief in Sight—All Schools Closed—Health Warning Issued

Disaster swept over the Triple Cities today on the crest of a flood unequalled in the history of the area.

Striking at all sections of the city, raging torrents of water mocked efforts of hundreds of workers who were waging a battle against almost insurmountable odds to protect the city from further damage.

With both the Susquehanna and Chenango rivers at the highest levels in history, a survey of the damage already registered revealed:

The city waterworks flooded, disabling all pumping equipment and leaving the city with water to last only one day.

A sand bag barricade at McDonald avenue swept away, pouring torrents of water into Front street, Gaines street, Valley street, Franklin street and Winding Way, flooding scores of homes.

The entire First Ward threatened with a worst disaster than that of last July if workers fighting to hold back the Chenango river with a sandbag barricade at Prospect street are unsuccessful in their fight.

A further rise in the rivers is predicted. Breaking of the barricade at McDonald avenue was expected to halt the rise in the water level of the Chenango river temporarily, but a further increase was expected this afternoon.

All seven bridges of the city are closed except the Memorial bridge, with the South Side completely isolated.

The Court street bridge is reported in danger of being swept away.

Hundreds of families are evacuating homes throughout flooded districts of Binghamton, Endicott and Johnson City.

The waterworks at the Binghamton State hospital is out of commission and hundreds of patients are being supplied from a reservoir containing approximately one day's supply.

The Endicott waterworks is about to be closed with only one day's supply available in reservoirs.

All highways leading into Binghamton closed to traffic.

Residents of the Triple Cities warned to boil all drinking water.

Only ten months after the flood of 1935, during the week of March 17, 1936, steady rains complicated the thawing of ice on the rivers and streams of central New York. Flooding began to occur over a wide-spread area of the state. Despite efforts to block the waters from escaping over the riverbanks, the water rose to more than two feet throughout most of Binghamton and the rest of the Triple Cities area. The waters caused the closing of all but one of the bridges into the city, and endangered the area's drinking water supply. When the waters subsided, the damage reports totaled $1.35 million. An outcry for adequate flood protection led to the construction of floodwalls along the rivers and the creation of the Whitney Point Reservoir. Courtesy of Binghamton City Historian

An aftermath of the floods of 1935 and 1936 was the construction of the bridge spanning the Chenango River near Clinton Street. The original structure was washed out in 1935 and a new structure begun, but the flood of 1936 caused major structural damage and the new bridge collapsed. Here workers inspect the remains of the bridge. From the Putnam Collection; courtesy of Broome County Public Library

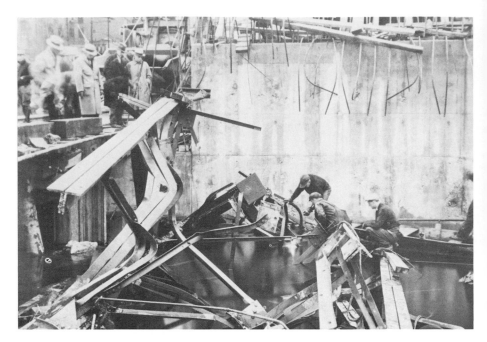

Misses & Children Lasting Room 100% for the E.J.aa 1/8/37

The employees of the Endicott-Johnson Corporation numbered in the thousands and included men and women from countries all over the world. Many employees worked for the firm for thirty, forty or even fifty years. It is difficult to find an older resident of the Triple Cities area who did not have a relative work for the company at some point. This photograph shows the workers of the Misses and Children's Factory in Johnson City (and includes the author's grandfather, William J. Webb). Courtesy of Gerald R. Smith

The statue of Daniel S. Dickinson was erected on Courthouse Square in 1924. The Universalist Church, now the site of the Binghamton Savings Bank, can be seen in the rear of the picture. From the Putnam Collection; courtesy of Broome County Public Library

A live model set this window display apart from others in 1937. Advertising the 1938 lineup of RCA radios, the display appeared in Weeks and Dickinson music store on

Chenango Street, and was a notable innovation to the downtown business scene. Courtesy of Broome County Historical Society

George F. Johnson with Franklin D. Roosevelt during FDR's tour of the area in 1937. George W. Johnson, George F.'s son, can be seen on the far right of the photograph. Courtesy of Broome County Historical Society

With the conclusion of the Second World War in 1945, the veteran came back to the valley with a sense of optimism that society would be able to prevent another such exercise in total destruction. New technology brought more efficiency in business and in the home, allowing a greater percentage of leisure time. Enterprising young men such as these two on Upper Front Street could sell their toys and hope to make enough money to buy a brand new Rollfast bicycle. Courtesy of Binghamton City Historian

Chapter Nine

From Smokestack to High-Tech
1941 to 1960

The outbreak of World War II brought further changes for the area. The industries of the local area had always employed a certain percentage of female workers, but with the large numbers of young men leaving to fight overseas, more women began to enter the job market. Many of the larger industries received government contracts to manufacture products to be used in the war effort. These contracts, like Endicott-Johnson's contract to manufacture army boots, helped improve the area's economy. In a controversial move, the federal government seized control of Agfa-Ansco, the local maker of cameras, because the parent company was German. The government would retain control of this business until the mid-1960s.

The veteran arrived back in the valley with a renewed sense of optimism and a hope for building a better future. Part of that future included a family, and the area experienced a baby boom during the late 1940s and early 1950s. The population of Binghamton eventually reached eighty-five thousand by the mid-1950s.

A secondary reaction to the returning veteran was the development of a higher education system that would provide college-level training for the former servicemen. The first institution to meet this need was Triple Cities College. It opened in 1946 in facilities provided jointly by the Endicott-Johnson Corporation and IBM and under the sponsorhip of Syracuse University. A year later a second college opened in Binghamton with an enrollment of 215 students. The New York State Institute of Applied Arts and Sciences was housed in the Government Armory on Washington Street and would soon change its name to Broome Technical Community College. It would later relocate to a new site in the town of Dickinson after a fire destroyed its first home.

The era of smokestack industry was slowly dying through-out the valley. Endicott-Johnson Corporation was beginning a long period of decline that would decrease the number of employees to less than half of its pre-war totals. The small mills and heavy industries of the first half of the twentieth century were being replaced by the "high-tech" industries such as Link, General Electric, Universal Instruments, and IBM.

The new type of industry was followed by a new lifestyle. No longer did life in the city have the appeal that it once did. The automobile had made travel back and forth to work relatively easy, and many people now considered the city dirty and noisy. A new word crept into the vocabulary—*suburbia*. The old adage about the grass being greener now seemed to be true, and that grass was not in Binghamton, but in Vestal, Kirkwood, Chenango Bridge, or Endicott. Greater numbers of people and businesses began the move to the outer reaches of the valley. Real estate costs were lower, and there was an ample supply of land that could be developed.

The city of Binghamton had seen its population reach its high point by the mid-1950s, and it now faced a long process of decline. But the city still held the monopoly on cultural institutions; Tri-Cities Opera began in 1948; the Binghamton Symphony started in 1953. A year later the Roberson Center for the Arts and Sciences became home to several constituent groups.

The city was also home to a new medium of communication: television. The first station, affiliated to WNBF radio, began broadcasts in 1949. If television was "a vast wasteland" as Newton Minow believed, it was also a medium that served to further the loss of a sense of community. One could watch the world happen on a small glass screen, rather than participate in events which evoked a feeling of being a part of the valley. The people of the valley were swiftly approaching a low point in the area's history.

The first planned park in the valley was a scene of peaceful solitude for many south side residents. In the early years of this century some residents persuaded Binghamton's government to purchase the land along the southern bank of the Susquehanna River to create a park on what was to have been the extension of the Chenango Canal. South Side Park gradually developed as a long narrow green area with a playground, bandstand (donated by George F. Johnson), and many monuments to the area's war dead. The bandstand was removed in 1968, but the park continues to commemorate the effort of local residents in wartime, and was rededicated as Veterans Park in 1987. From the Putnam Collection; courtesy of Broome County Public Library

Vaudeville shows may have passed away after the end of the war, but the movie was still popular diversion. Parents could give their children a nickel and tell them to go to the theater and watch the latest serial of Gene Autry or Hopalong Cassidy. The biggest theater in the area was the Capitol on Exchange Street in Binghamton. Constructed in the 1920s, the theater could hold well over one thousand people, and originally presented vaudeville shows. The theater was torn down in the early 1960s to make room for a parking lot for the Binghamton Savings Bank next to the theater. From the Putnam Collection; courtesy of Broome County Public Library

186

Children near the memorial gardens at South Side Park. From the Putnam Collection; courtesy of Broome County Public Library

A World War I memorial in South Side Park. From the Putnam Collection; courtesy of Broome County Public Library

The park on Mount Prospect donated by S. Mills Ely was turned into a municipal golf course for all residents to enjoy. For many years this entrance to the park on Prospect Street, followed by a long flight of stairs, was a familiar sight to the area. The gateway was removed in 1968 to make way for the Route 17 expansion. Courtesy of Broome County Historical Society

During the late 1940s the empire that once was Willis Sharpe Kilmer's slowly began disappearing. Sun Briar Court had been the pride of the Riverside Drive area, costing a million dollars and representing the best that money could buy. By the 1940s and 1950s the stables were little used, and the land comprising the complex was sold off for residential and commercial development. The clubhouse of the stables is today owned by Lourdes Hospital, and little else of the complex remains. This aerial view shows the expanse of the facility, with two tracks and the stables in the center of the picture. From Bob Garvin collection; courtesy of Broome County Historical Society

"Play ball" was a familiar cry at the baseball games that were attended by thousands at Johnson Field in Johnson City. The stadium was the home of the Triplets baseball team. A minor league team sponsored by the New York Yankees, the Triplets produced many players who would go on to major league careers, like Whitey Ford and Thurman Munson. Johnson Field, seen in this aerial photograph, was torn down in the mid-1960s when the Route 17 expressway needed room for expansion. From the Bob Garvin Collection; courtesy of Broome County Historical Society

Thousands of returning veterans needed education and training and the area responded by creating two colleges. The New York State Institute for Applied Arts and Sciences opened in 1947, one year after Triple Cities College began in Endicott in George F. Johnson's donated home, and on land given by IBM. The New York Institute (pictured) began in the Washington Street Armory in Binghamton, soon changing its name to Broome Technical Community College. The armory caught fire and burned down in 1952, and the school moved down "Fraternity Row" to the Kalurah Temple and operated out of the structure until a new site for the college was chosen in the town of Dickinson in 1954. Courtesy of Broome County Historical Society

As Broome Technical Community College grew on Upper Front Street, so did the number of buildings for the students attending the school. This early photograph of the college shows the original "quad" of buildings that became Broome Community College. Now part of the State University of New York system of colleges, the school has over seven thousand part-time and full-time students. Aerial photograph by Bob Garvin; courtesy of Binghamton City Historian

On November 10, 1947, the Freedom Train pulled into the railroad station in Binghamton for one stop on its journey around the country. The train's cars were filled with displays and exhibits of the memorabilia that were part of this country's heritage. Thousands of people came to view this once-in-a-lifetime chance to see documents that shaped a nation's destiny or items used by famous Americans. Thirty years later another Freedom Train would be sent around the country in honor of the United States' Bicentennial. The familiar shape of the old gas tank is seen in the rear of the photograph. Photograph by John Warner; courtesy of Binghamton City Historian

A gift of a lifetime was the donation of six carousels to the area's residents by George F. Johnson and the Johnson family. This area has more carousels for the size of the population than any other location in the country. When George F. was a small child he was denied a ride on a carousel because he did not have any money. Because of this memory, his donations to the community stipulate that the carousels shall be forever free to the people of the region. This photograph from 1956 shows employees of the Binghamton Parks Department who had recently repainted the horses on the carousel at Ross Park. The carousels have deteriorated in recent years, and efforts have begun to preserve and protect them from further damage. Photograph by the Evening Press; courtesy of Broome County Historical Society

The dawn of a new age approached with the broadcast of the area's first television show in 1949. The show was an interview with Binghamton's Mayor Donald Kramer. The program was hosted by Tom Cawley, then a writer for the Binghamton Press, who would gain local fame as a columnist describing everyday life in the valley for the next thirty years. Television aided in bringing the world into the homes of the citizens and started a long process of isolating them from the activities that had made them a part of the community. Courtesy of Binghamton City Historian

The five and ten cent store reached its height of popularity in the 1950s. Shoppers could find almost anything they wanted, and bargains and sales could lead to a rush of customers trying to beat each other for the best buy. Kresge's was a staple of downtown Binghamton for many years. Situated across the corner from its competitor, Woolworth's, the store offered a variety of goods. The store would change names and become the Jupiter Store in the early 1960s and close by the end of that decade, but the firm was restructured and today is the parent company of the K-Mart chain of stores. From the Lester Lee Cole collection; courtesy of Broome County Historical Society

In 1954 a new airfield was constructed on the top of Mount Ettrick to handle the increasing numbers of flights into the Broome County area. The Broome County Airport replaced the old Bennett Field site, and, along with Tri-Cities Airport, continues to provide valu- able air service to the area as the Edwin A. Link Field. The sight of a Mohawk Airplane on the landing strips of the airport during the 1950s was familiar to local residents. Courtesy of Broome County Historical Society

The old tuberculosis hospital in the Chenango Bridge area was transformed into a nursing home during this period. The facility was at first an independent agency, but it was later taken over by the Broome County government along with the Willow Point facility in an effort to bring better service to the elderly of the community. The home continues to operate today. From the Bob Garvin collection; courtesy of Broome County Historical Society

As the Asylum for the Chronically Insane became the Binghamton State Hospital (and finally the Binghamton Psychiatric Center) during this century, the treatment for the patients also improved. Mental illness was seen as treatable, and new facilities were constructed to house the residents and provide for their well-being. The Garvin building, pictured, was the largest and most recent addition to the complex and represented the state-of-the-art during the 1950s. From the Bob Garvin collection; courtesy of Broome County Historical Society

The First Congregational Church on the corner of Front and Main streets in Binghamton was constructed on the site which once was home to Peterson's Tavern. The congregation has occupied this site since 1863, and the main portion of the present structure was erected at that time. Newer additions have increased the size of the church, and the back portion of the church in this 1958 photograph was replaced by a newer building. From the Lester Lee Cole collection; courtesy of Broome County Historical Society

A symbol of times gone by is the gas tank that once graced the east side of Binghamton. Its familiar shape was a beacon to residents returning home. This 1959 photograph of the tank shows its reflection in the waters of the Susquehanna River next to the Tompkins Street bridge. The tank was built in 1927 as part of the Columbia Gas Company complex and was removed in 1969. Courtesy of Broome County Historical Society

Chapter Ten

Twilight of the Valley
1960 to 1976

In the fall of 1960 the voters of the country chose between Richard Nixon, the vice president of the United States under Dwight Eisenhower, and John F. Kennedy, a young Democratic senator from Massachusetts who spoke of a new vision for America as a world leader. The election of Kennedy reinforced the image of the nation as a progressive, modern society in which each citizen would have the opportunity to climb the ladder of success.

But from the cities of the country where urban blight was becoming increasingly noticeable, to the distant shores of a small country in Southeast Asia where civil war raged, there were signs of changes in the American way of life. An assassin's bullet on November 22, 1963, cut short the life of the thirty-fifth president, ended the era of Camelot that the century had felt, and catapulted the nation into an era of violence, civil unrest, student protests, and great change in the structure of society.

In the valley a new look took shape in 1960 when the Susquehanna River was rechanneled in the Endwell area to make way for the construction of Route 17. The Southern Tier Expressway, as Route 17 became known, and the Penn-Can Highway (Interstate 81) tied the area together in a ribbon of concrete that made travel throughout the state more efficient, but was disruptive to the neighborhoods and businesses that stood in its way. Entire streets of homes were eliminated, and institutions such as Johnson Field were torn down to make way for the new roadways.

Near the new highways a phenomenon called the shopping plaza was created to lure residents into a self-contained area of stores and restaurants. In 1961 the Stow Flats area of Bingham-

ton was filled in and Binghamton Plaza was added to the landscape. The phenomenon continued to expand to the towns of Vestal, Chenango, and Union, and with this expansion businesses that had been traditionally the staples of Binghamton began to feel the strain of a new form of competition. By 1963 Sisson Brothers and Weldon Department Store had closed and the population of Binghamton, which had peaked in the mid-1950s, was on the decline.

The tanneries of the Endicott-Johnson Corporation, which had operated for sixty-four years, closed, and the firm which had been part of the Johnson family for many years was sold to an outside firm by the latter part of the decade. The look of downtown Binghamton was considered by many to have a tired and worn look, and plans were conceived to modernize the appearance by removing many of the older structures and replacing them with new buildings.

The concept of "urban renewal" spread throughout much of the country. Federal and state monies were made available to remove the buildings and plan for new construction. The difficulty with the program was that the funds needed to rebuild on the now vacant lots were not there and many cities, like Binghamton, began to look like London after the bombings of World War II.

To the west of Binghamton, Johnson City grew in size with the annexations of Westover and Oakdale, while Harper College, which had located to lands along the newly built Vestal Parkway became the State University of New York at Binghamton. The new center of undergraduate and graduate study would continue to expand and grow for the next two decades. On Upper Front Street in the Town of Dickinson, Broome Technical Community College adopted a new liberal arts program and became Broome Community College.

Television brought the horrible images of death and destruction of the Vietnam War into the home of each citizen, and the unrest on the nation's campuses was felt throughout the country. It seemed that the land was being split apart under the flood of change. Increased unrest over the civil rights struggle, over equal rights for all persons regardless of sex, and even over the length of one's hair only furthered the division.

"A city on the verge of change" could be the caption for this 1960 photograph. As the population of Binghamton moved toward the suburbs, so did many of the businesses. Link relocated to Kirkwood, General Electric was in Westover, and this area's first shopping plaza, the Binghamton Plaza, was about to open on Stow Flats. The old city looked tired and the buildings were thought by many to be bleak and unappealing. From the Valley Development Foundation collection; courtesy of Binghamton City Historian

A lack of confidence was felt in the land. For the first time in America's history, a president resigned the office under the threat of almost certain impeachment for obstruction of justice in the Watergate affair. This lack of confidence was also felt in the valley. Businesses which had been a part of Binghamton history for nearly a century moved out of their downtown stores and into the newly constructed Oakdale Mall, which opened in 1975. A shrinking tax base forced larger and larger increases in taxes to maintain the services that Binghamton residents demanded from their municipal government.

The feeling of community, which had once been so strong, was ebbing toward a new low. The activities that had once been a drawing card to the area's citizens—the Triplets, the parks, outdoor activities sponsored by the Endicott-Johnson Corporation, and downtown movie theaters, were now gone.

The close of the 1960s, however, brought renewed hope for the area. The construction of a joint Government Complex that would house the offices for the governments of Binghamton, Broome County, and New York State was opened in 1973. In that same year Edwin Crawford became the first county executive under the newly reorganized county government. The first phase of Woodburn Court housing for the elderly and low-income groups was completed.

New cultural groups such as the B. C. Pops began to draw people back to the region. The B. C. Open began in 1971, and the Kopernick Observatory was opened in the hills of Vestal in 1974. In 1975 the Broome County Center for the Performing Arts was begun in the old Capri (originally the Binghamton) Theatre. More commonly called the Forum, the center provided a home for the Tri-Cities Opera, the Binghamton Symphony, the B. C. Pops organizations, and other theater and dance groups.

As the nation prepared to celebrate its Bicentennial, a renewed sense of hope and purpose pulled the nation and the people of the valley away from the disruptive influences of the previous decade and toward a new beginning.

A problem that still plagues residents of the Triple Cities. Proposed solutions to the flooding have been around nearly as long as the underpasses that cause it. Courtesy of Broome County Historical Society

The shape of things to come could be seen in the new municipal building constructed in 1960 in Endicott. The older buildings were viewed as outdated, and it was thought that only new buildings could help update the look of the area. Courtesy of Broome County Historical Society

A favorite son of Binghamton, Rod Serling (1924-1975) came to this area from Syracuse when he was two years old. He graduated from Binghamton's Central High School and entered the world of writing full-time shortly after he completed college. His best known work was "Twilight Zone," which he created and hosted. But that was only one part of his notable career. He won several Emmys and a number of other awards, and was teaching at Ithaca College when he died from heart disease in 1975. Courtesy of Broome County Historical Society

In a celebration of the area's newspaper history, Ruth Clanhan, a staff member from Roberson Center, is shown surrounded by some of the newspapers that have brought the day's events to the valley's residents. The first newspaper, the American Constellation, *began in 1800. At the time this photograph was taken, the area still had two independent newspapers, the* Sun-Bulletin *and the* Evening Press. *They would shortly merge under the common ownership of the Gannett Corporation. Courtesy of Broome County Historical Society*

The era of fast food began in the Triple Cities in 1963, when the first McDonald's opened across from the Binghamton Plaza on State Street. More and more fast food restaurants and stores would cluster in areas like State Street and the Vestal Parkway. Courtesy of Broome County Historical Society

A "sign" of the times is this photograph of the urban sprawl that spread along the Vestal Parkway beginning in the 1960s. The opening of the State University campus and several shopping plazas on that highway only added to the blur of advertisements that bombarded the motorist from every angle. Courtesy of Broome County Historical Society

A well-known figure in local broadcasting, Ralph Carroll began his career in the early years of radio and along with Edwin Weeks was one of the top broadcasters for many years. He would later make the transition to that new medium, television, hosting his own show, "Carroll's Caravan." Courtesy of Broome County Historical Society

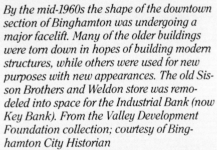

By the mid-1960s the shape of the downtown section of Binghamton was undergoing a major facelift. Many of the older buildings were torn down in hopes of building modern structures, while others were used for new purposes with new appearances. The old Sisson Brothers and Weldon store was remodeled into space for the Industrial Bank (now Key Bank). From the Valley Development Foundation collection; courtesy of Binghamton City Historian

The old Kresge-Jupiter store under renovations to shortly become Chase Bank, which has since closed. From the Valley Development Foundation collection; courtesy of Binghamton City Historian

In 1965 Johnson City celebrated its seventy-fifth anniversary as a village. One of the many dignitaries to join in the festivities was Robert Kennedy, then New York State's junior senator. He is seen here greeting some of the local participants. Courtesy of Your Home Library

In the late 1960s Endicott built a new library on the site of the original building. Despite some protests about removing George F. Johnson's home (which had been given to the village as the Ideal Library by the Johnson family), the new library opened on Park Street in a modern, efficiently designed structure. Courtesy of Broome County Historical Society

In 1965 the Triple Cities College was renamed the State University of New York Center at Binghamton. The college had started in 1946 in Endicott as an adjunct to Syracuse University, but by the late 1950s it had outgrown the Quonset hut classrooms and offices, and moved to a larger space along the Vestal Parkway. The main college of the university was named in honor of Robert Harpur, one of New York's early educators and major area landowners. Today the university has more than ten thousand full-time students, and is ranked among the top state universities in the nation. From the Bob Garvin collection; courtesy of Broome County Historical Collection

Binghamton celebrated its centennial as a city in the fall of 1967 with the unveiling of its new official flag, designed by a local high school student, and an elaborate cake cutting ceremony, with Mayor Joseph Esworthy doing the honors. Courtesy of Broome County Historical Society

Speeches, fanfare and frosting were all a part of Binghamton's centennial celebration. Courtesy of Broome County Historical Society

As part of the urban renewal process of the late 1960s and early 1970s the rivers began once again to play a part in the community. Efforts were made to beautify them with promenades. The Martin Luther King, Jr. Promenade, named in 1986, graces the eastern bank of the Chenango River. Courtesy of Binghamton City Historian

Centennial Plaza was the name given to this green area surrounded by Henry and Chenango streets. The John F. Kennedy Memorial monument, erected in 1967, adorns this site adjacent to 100 Chenango Place. Courtesy of Broome County Public Library

A ribbon of concrete began to encircle the Triple Cities in the 1960s and 1970s. Interstate 81 (also known as the Penn-Can Highway) and Routes 17 and 88 eased the flow of traffic through the region. During the course of construction, many well-known structures were demolished, and entire neighborhoods were uprooted. The cloverleaf of Route 81 near the Brandywine Highway can be seen in this view. Photograph by Bob Garvin; courtesy of Binghamton City Historian

The need for a more modern downtown increased in the late 1960s. A governmental center that would provide space for Binghamton, Broome County, and New York State's offices was planned for the area south of Court Street. This same area was to be home to the new headquarters for the First City National Bank, the Marine Midland Bank, and a civic auditorium built as a memorial to the men who died in the Second World War. This aerial view shows the clearing of several blocks of land and the construction of the North Shore Drive connector and the expansion of the Collier Street (now State Street) bridge. Aerial photograph by Bob Garvin; courtesy of Binghamton City Historian

The land next to the J. C. Penney store was cleared of the old buildings and the old Police Station in the rear of the photograph was about to be torn down to make way for new construction. From the Valley Development Foundation collection; courtesy of Binghamton City Historian

The downtown took shape during the 1960s, with the construction of the Government Complex under way and the opening of the Treadway Inn (now the Holiday Inn-Arena). The Marine Midland Plaza building was under construction as the valley entered the 1970s, and the new First City National Bank was no longer an architect's model, but a reality. But there were serious problems as well. Much of Binghamton still lacked any new buildings where structures had previously stood, and many of the businesses that had been displaced by the modernization of the area either left the city or went out of business entirely. Aerial photograph by Bob Garvin; courtesy of Binghamton City Historian.

Opening ceremonies for the Treadway Inn. From the Valley Development Foundation collection; courtesy of Binghamton City Historian

The Treadway Inn is completed and the Marine Midland Bank building begins to take shape behind it. From the Valley Development Foundation collection; courtesy of Binghamton City Historian

Architect's model of the First City National Bank. From the Valley Development Foundation collection; courtesy of Binghamton City Historian

The declining student population during the 1970s closed many schools and left the problem of empty buildings. The solution was different in the various parts of the valley. In the city of Binghamton the Daniel Dickinson School in the First Ward was closed. Too expensive to maintain as a nonfunctioning school, the building (which housed a branch of the Binghamton Public Library) was torn down in the early 1970s. From the Valley Development Foundation collection; courtesy of Binghamton City Historian

Unlike the Daniel Dickinson School seen at top and at right, in Johnson City a new high school was under construction near the site of the future Oakdale Mall. Rather than tear down the old high school, it was sold for use as commercial space under the name of the NY-Penn Trading Center. It was the beginning of a trend which was slowly gaining momentum in the area, rehabilitation rather than destruction. From the Valley Development Foundation collection; courtesy of Binghamton City Historian

A snowy day in Binghamton brought few cars to the new parking ramps constructed to attract shoppers. Despite noble attempts at luring patrons back to the city, the free parking of the shopping plazas and malls still held the attention of many of the residents. By the early 1970s an exodus of retail stores, including Sears, Montgomery Wards, Fowlers, Compton-Dunns, and the closing of McLeans, seriously hurt the viability of Binghamton's place as the strongest link in the Triple Cities. From the Valley Development Foundation collection; courtesy of Binghamton City Historian   .

Interstate 81 & Route 17

Northshore Drive

Susquehanna River

K

J

L

A

B

M

C

N

N

D

F

I

E

H

N

G

Chenango River

By the nation's Bicentennial in 1976 the face
of the Triple Cities had begun to take on its
present appearance. This aerial view of
Binghamton, used in planning future devel-
opments, shows the extent of new construction by the mid-1970s. New parking ramps,
office buildings, and housing for the elderly
and low-income groups had been completed.
The future MetroCenter would be constructed
on the empty blocks along Court, Washington, and State streets by the early 1980s.
From the Valley Development Foundation
collection; courtesy of Binghamton City
Historian

Chapter Eleven

A New Day Begins
1976 to 1988

The harbor of New York was filled with the sight of tall ships, their sails waving as if in salute to Lady Liberty. The year was 1976 and the country was basking in the warmth of its Bicentennial festivities. It seemed that suddenly patriotism was no longer an obsolete theme, but one which had real meaning in the operation of our government and lives.

If it appeared that the sun had set on the valley during the previous period, there now seemed to be the hint of a new light upon the horizon. Although the retail markets of Binghamton had changed rapidly in the early years of the 1970s with the departure of Fowlers, Montgomery Ward, Sears, and the closing of McLeans, the strength of the Oakdale Mall and other shopping plazas helped to maintain the changing markets.

A new interest was shown in revitalizing the older structures of the region. Rather than tear down the old, it was reasoned that it might be cheaper and more visually pleasing to rehabilitate older homes and buildings for contemporary uses. McFarland-Johnson Engineering took a nineteenth-century home and renovated it into a viable working headquarters. The old Stephens paper factory on State Street was converted into retail and office space. The City Hall building on Collier Street became Best Western's Hotel DeVille. The Rounds estate in Vestal was converted into the Drover's Inn, and the Davidge mansion across from the Roberson Center was restored for law offices.

The industrial heritage of this community was celebrated by the selection of the Triple Cities as one site in the new concept of Urban Parks created in New York State. The Susquehanna Urban Cultural Park was conceived to promote the history of the area's businesses, and centers for the new program were established at the newly renovated Lackawanna Station and in Your Home Library in Johnson City.

In 1979 the Broome County Industrial Incubator was created in facilities once owned by the Endicott-Johnson Corporation and helped to spur the growth of smaller businesses. The growth of the Kirkwood Industrial Park continued, and its success aided in forming the plans for the creation of the new Conklin Industrial Park.

The decade of the 1980s was not without its problems. For the first time since the creation of Broome County, its population declined. The exodus of people from Binghamton had taken its toll on the entire community, and many residents realized that the loss in one area of the region had a profound effect on the rest of the area. In 1981 a fire in the State Office Building spewed much more than just smoke and ash throughout the complex. Deadly PCB's and dioxins were released and the problem of cleaning the facility compelled the people of the area to work together to alleviate the problem. The transformer fire in that building only pointed out the increasingly complex problems that modern society presented. The need for safe and adequate removal of garbage, the removal of the pollution from the air, land, and water, and the need for affordable housing for the elderly, and low-income groups were only a few of the difficulties that faced the community.

We live in a region that has seen the arrival of the canal, the railroad, the automobile, and the airplane. Our industries now produce the computer chips an aeronautical devices which will take man to the stars. Thousands of immigrants came to this small valley nestled along the banks of the Chenango and Susquehanna rivers to live and work. Their diverse ethnic heritages have not been lost in some vague attempt to make them "American," but are proudly maintained and preserved as a vital link to our past. The richness of our land is enriched by the richness of our people. Like the people that once inhabited this land, we have come to realize that we can only survive by working together. The revitalization of our area continues to expand and take new directions. The valley has again become a valley of opportunity.

A new concept in industrial growth occurred with the creation of the Broome County Industrial Incubator. The incubator used the old Endicott-Johnson Athletic Association building near Main Street in Johnson City as a spot where small businesses unable to afford regular sites could operate until they had enough capital to move into other facilities. One of the most successful companies that began in the incubator is Ebonex, which has grown into a multi-million dollar company which now occupies the site formerly used by Brewer-Tichener in Binghamton and plans a major expansion in the near future. Courtesy of Broome County Historical Society

While Binghamton tried to change the look of its downtown, Johnson City began an effort to preserve its small town look. A tradition in the Johnson City area was the Crystal Tea Room on Main Street. This photograph from the Evening Press in 1977 shows the classic diner-like atmosphere combined with a menu of good food. Although somewhat changed today, the Crystal Restaurant still operates from the same location. Courtesy of Broome County Historical Society

From the offices of the politicians in the new Government Complex in Binghamton came a new look at the community that they lived in. no longer could Binghamton consider itself isolated from the rest of the community. The creation of the Oakdale Mall in 1975 represented the culmination in forces that had successfully pulled away business and people from the area. Although Binghamton's population had been decreasing since the mid-1950s, the remaining towns in Broome County had absorbed most of the movement out of the city. For the first time in 1980 the population of the entire region dropped. The loss of the marketplace in Binghamton had begun to affect the rest of the community. A new philosophy was needed. From the Valley Development Foundation collection; courtesy of Binghamton City Historian

Another view of the Government Center. From the Valley Development Foundation collection; courtesy of Binghamton City Historian

Sculpture in front of the new City Hall at the Government Center. From the Valley Development Foundation collection; courtesy of Binghamton City Historian

Both old and new buildings represented the various types of industries that once flourished in the Triple Cities. A new era of cooperation was required to solve many of the difficult problems that modern society was creating. One of these problems occurred after a transformer fire occurred in the State Office Building (tall building at right of photo) in the Government Complex in February 1981. The fire released deadly PCB's and dioxins throughout the eighteen stories of the building. Cooperation between the government agencies and the community to establish a clean-up procedure for what became known as the "toxic tower" aided in resolving the problem. From the Valley Development Foundation collection; courtesy of Binghamton City Historian

A new phrase—historic preservation—began to intrigue community leaders. The concept of reusing older structures rather than tearing them down was attractive. It offered a refurbished building at less than the cost of new construction, and allowed for the preservation of attractive architectural features that could no longer be duplicated. One of the early leaders in this effort was James Mowry, who began with this building at 180 State Street, shown at left, and continued by working on the Stephen's Square building (below, which once housed a paper factory and later, George Kent's cigar business) and the Stephen's Square Marketplace. His efforts inspired others to participate in restoration, and today the Hotel De Ville occupies the old City Hall, a historic district has been created in downtown Binghamton, while Drover's Inn recently opened in an 1840 era tavern in Vestal. State Street photograph from the Valley Development Foundation collection; courtesy of Binghamton City Historian. Stephen's Square photograph courtesy of Broome County Historical Society

In 1984 Governor Mario Cuomo visited Binghamton during its sesquicentennial celebration. A new outlook had begun. Boscov's department store opened in the empty Fowler's building in that same year and MetroCenter would open a year later. The retail structure of the Binghamton area was improving. The Oakdale Mall continued to thrive, and new areas of retail space were being created throughout the valley. A stronger sense of community was promoted in the Triple Cities area. Mayor Juanita Crabb of Binghamton can be seen on the far left of this photograph. Photograph by Kathleen Mezzadonna; courtesy of Binghamton City Historian

New housing around the Triple Cities has aided in bringing people back to the area. Public housing such as Woodburn Court, Ely Park, and Saratoga Terrace, shown here, were constructed. Courtesy of Broome County Historical Society

New homes for middle-class families such as those recently completed in Binghamton's First Ward and projects completed on the north side of the city and on the site of the old Daniel Dickinson School, have created a renaissance in the area's neighborhoods. *Courtesy of Broome County Historical Society*

This area has always been a composite of the old and the new. It encourages the differences between the many ethnic groups that make up our population. Washingtonian Hall, built in 1799 in Endwell and still standing in excellent condition near the modern IBM factories which produce computers that are revolutionizing the way we operate our society, serves as a symbol of the diversity within the valley. *Photograph by John Warner; courtesy of Binghamton City Historian*

The rivers provide the region with a source of water, a means of transportation, and a connection between the various areas within the valley. The small communities that grew along these rivers were tied together by a common bond. Roads, canals, and railroads brought the people of the valley even closer to each other. The differences that separate us seem very slight when looking down from above. Even in a photograph from the 1950s it is hard to tell where Binghamton ends and Johnson City begins, or where Vestal, Endicott, and Endwell stop or start. This difference is even less today. The valley has never been a region of distinct entities, but one of continuous growth and settlement. As the people of the region experience a reawakening of their community's heritage, the sun once again rises on the valley of opportunity. Photograph by Bob Garvin; courtesy of Binghamton City Historian

Bibliography

BOOKS AND ARTICLES

Alberts, Robert C. *The Golden Voyage: The Life and Times of William Bingham, 1752-1804*. Boston: Houghton, Mifflin Company, 1969.

Art Work of Binghamton in Nine Parts. Binghamton, Chicago: Gravure Illustration Company, 1902.

Binghamton Board of Trade. *Industrial Binghamton, 1900-1901*. Binghamton, New York: 1901.

Binghamton Chamber of Commerce. *The Valley of Opportunity*. Binghamton, New York: Charles W. Baldwin, 1920.

Binghamton Illustrated. Binghamton, New York: H. R. Page and Company, 1890.

Binghamton, Past and Present: Its Commerce, Trade and Industries, Descriptive and Historical. Binghamton, New York: The Evening Herald Company, 1894.

Bothwell, Lawrence. *Broome County Heritage: An Illustrated History*. Woodland Hills, CA: Windsor Publications, 1983.

Byrne, Thomas E. *A Bicentennial Remembrance of the Sullivan-Clinton Expedition, 1779*. Elmira, New York: Sullivan-Clinton '79, New York State Bicentennial Commission, and Chemung County Historical Society, 1979.

Combination Atlas Map of Broome County, New York. Philadelphia: Everts, Ensign and Everts, 1876.

Elliott, Dolores. "Otseningo, an Example of an Eighteenth Century Settlement Pattern." *Current Perspectives in Northeastern Archeology: Essays in Honor of William A. Ritchie*. Robert E. Funk and Charles F. Hayes, ed. III, 93-105. Rochester and Albany, New York: New York State Archeological Association, 1977.

Ellis, David M., James A. Frost, Harold C. Syrett, and Harry J. Carman. *A History of New York State*. Ithaca, New York: Cornell University Press, 1967.

Endicott-Johnson Corporation. *Partners All: A Pictorial Narrative of an Industrial Democracy*. Photographs by Russell C. Aikins. New York: Huntington Corporation, 1938.

Fiori, James V. *A History of Endicott*. Endicott, New York: James V. Fiori, 1982.

Graymont, Barbara. *The Iroquois in the American Revolution*. Syracuse, New York: Syracuse University Press, 1972.

Hinman, Marjory B. *Court House Square: A Social History*. Endicott, New York: Marjory B. Hinman, 1984.

_____. *Lost Landmarks of Broome County*. Endicott, New York: Marjory B. Hinman, 1983.

_____. *Onaquaga: Hub of the Border Wars*. Binghamton, New York: Marjory B. Hinman, 1975.

Hopkins, Joseph G. E., ed. *Concise Dictionary of American Biography*. New York: Charles Scribner and Sons, 1964.

Inglis, William. *George F. Johnson and His Industrial Democracy*. New York: Huntington Press, 1935.

Kelsay, Isabel Thompson. *Joseph Brandt, 1743-1804, Man of Two Worlds*. Syracuse, New York: Syracuse University Press, 1984.

King, Sheldon S. *Trolleys of the Triple Cities*. Interlaken, New York: Heart of the Lakes Publishing, 1987.

Lawyer, William S., ed. *Binghamton, Its Settlement, Growth and Development*. n.p.: Century Memorial Publishing Company, 1900.

Lewis, Georgina. *William Bingham (1752-1804): Speculator on America*. Binghamton, New York: Broome County Historical Society, 1974.

McGuire, Ross and Nancy Grey Osterud. *Working Lives: Broome County, New York, 1800-1930*. Binghamton, New York: Roberson Center for the Arts and Sciences, 1980.

Montillon, Eugene D. *Historic Architecture in Broome County, New York and Vicinity*. Binghamton, New York: Broome County Planning Department and Broome County Historical Society, 1972.

O'Callaghan, E. B., ed. *The Documentary History of the State of New York*. 4 vols. Albany: n.p., 1849-1851.

Ritchie, William A. *"Algonquin-Iroquois Contact Site on Castle Creek, New York"*. Research Records of the Rochester Municipal Museum, no. 2. Rochester, New York: University of Rochester, 1934.

Seward, William Foote, ed. *Binghamton and Broome County, New York: A History*. 3 vols. New York: Lewis Historical Publishing Company, 1924.

Smith, Gerald R. "The Liberty Line and Southern New York: The Underground Railroad in Broome, Tioga, and Chemung Counties" n.p., 1979.

_____. *The People's University: A History of Binghamton Library Societies and the Binghamton Public Library*. Binghamton, New York: Gerald R. Smith, 1980.

Smith, H. P., ed. *History of Broome County*. Syracuse, New York: D. Mason and Company, 1885.

Stone, William. *Life of Brant and the Border Wars*. 2 vols. Albany: Munsell, 1838.

Versaggi, Nina M. *Hunter to Farmer: 10,000 Years of Susquehanna Prehistory*. Binghamton, New York: Roberson Center for the Arts and Sciences, 1986.

Wilkinson, J. B. *J. B. Wilkinson's The Annals of Binghamton of 1840*. Binghamton, New York: The Broome County Historical Society and the Old Onaquaga Historical Society, 1967.

MANUSCRIPT COLLECTIONS

Putnam, Dr. Frederick, comp. *A Documentary History of Broome County*. 126 vols. Broome County Public Library, Binghamton, New York.

Index

A

Alms House, 70
American House, 166
Arlington Hotel, 164

B

Bennett, Abel, 55
Bennett Field, 177
Bingham, Anne, 23
Bingham, William, 21, 22
Bingham Patent, 21, 22, 24, 25
Binghamton Academy, 49
Binghamton Asylum for the Chronically
    Insane, 71, 192
Binghamton Chair Company, 84
Binghamton Driving Park Association, 69
Binghamton gas works, 81
Binghamton High School, 116
Binghamton Lager Beer Brewery, 61
Binghamton Public Library, 124, 125
Binghamton Wagon Works, 63, 64
Binghamton Water Cure, 60
Binghamton water works, 80
Bingos, 99
Blanchard and Bartlett Planing Mill,
    44, 45
Brandt, Joseph, 20, 21
Brigham, Elizah, 100
Broome, Col. John, 22, 28
Broome Community College, 185, 189
Broome County Courthouse, 22, 33, 54,
    117, 154, 155
Broome County Incubator, 211, 212
Broome County Jail, 54
Broome County Poor House, 70
Brown, Dr. Titus home, 82
Bundy, Harlow, 96, 152
Bundy Manufacturing Company, 75, 96

C

CFJ Park, 168, 169
Capitol Theater, 186

Carousels, 190
Carroll, Ralph, 199
Casey, Daniel, 140
Castle Creek, 10, 11, 12, 13, 14, 15, 16
Chapman, Orlow, 124
Chenango Canal, 35, 36, 37, 38, 39,
    44, 46, 65
Chenango Point, 27
Chenango Silk Factory, 162
Christ Church, 42
Cigar making, 74, 75, 88, 89, 90, 91,
    92, 130
Civil War, 35, 50, 51, 80
Collier, John, 34, 36
Columbia bicycle, 83
Commercial Travellers Home, 110
Crandal and Stone, 63
Crowley Foods, 175
Cutler Ice Company, 147

D

Dickinson, Daniel S., 29, 35, 42
Dr. Doan's Sanitarium, 93
Duke's School, Mrs., 70
Dwight, Walton, 62
Dwight Block, 62

E

Ely, S. Mills, 110, 128
Empire Theatre, 129
Endicott, 75, 119, 127, 144, 152, 153,
    165, 170, 171, 185, 197, 201, 217
Endicott-Johnson Corporation, 75, 127,
    136, 158, 162, 167, 182
Endicott Trust Company, 97

F

Faatz Brush and Felting Works, 102
Fairbanks Valve Company, 132
Fairplay Caramels, 150
Fairview Home, 73
Felters Company, 102

Fire Departments, 64, 66, 78, 79, 104
Fireman's Hall, 55
First Congregational Church, 33, 193
First Baptist Church, 43
Flook, William E., 16
Floods, 157, 178, 179, 180, 181, 182
Fowler, Dick and Walker, 137

G
GAF, 176
Gaige, Egbert Home, 72
George F. Johnson Memorial Library, 201
Goudey Station, 161

H
Hand, Dr. Stephan D., 43
Harmony Seminary, 58
Hawley, Gideon, 18
Hill, William, 159
Hills, McLeans, and Haskins, 97
Homeopathic Medicine, 43
Hospitals, 86, 147, 154, 155, 174
Hotel Frederick, 119
House of Good Shephard, 73

I
IBM, 96, 127, 152, 153, 157, 185
Ideal Park, 148, 149
Indian settlement, 10, 11, 12, 13, 14, 15,
    16, 17, 18, 19, 20, 21
International Time Recording
    Company, 96
Iroquois pottery, 14, 15, 16

J
Johnson, C. Fred, 158
Johnson, George F., 75, 127, 141, 143,
    152, 163, 183
Johnson, Sir William, 11, 12, 19, 20, 21
Johnson City, 127, 158, 161, 166, 167,
    168, 169, 200, 212
Johnson Field, 189

Jones, Gen. Edward F., 57
Jones Scale Works, 57

K
Kilmer, Jonas, 94
Kilmer, Wilis Sharpe, 95
Kilmer and Company, 94, 95
Ku Klux Klan, 157, 166

L
Lady Jane Grey School, 76
Lestershire, 75, 101, 102, 103, 104, 105,
    121, 122, 123, 127, 135
Link, Edwin A., 157, 172, 173
Link Company, 157, 172, 173

M
Major House, 59
Marshall Furniture Company, 134
Memorial Bridge, 161
Mercereau, Major David, 59
Milks and Watson, 63
Millsville, 47
Monday Afternoon Club, 111
Morgan House, 44
Morning Sun, 131

N
New York State Inebriate Asylum, 53, 71
Nineteen Hundred Washer Company, 108
Noyes Comb Factory, 84

O
Old Bay Tom, 65
Onaquaga, 11, 12, 17, 18
Orton, Dr. John, 67
Otseningo, 11, 12, 17

P
Perry, Isaac, 71, 97, 111, 142
Peterson Tavern, 29, 33
Phelps Bank building, 142

Police departments, 78, 111
Port Dickinson, 39
Post office, 118
Powell Coal Company, 137
Press Building, 125

Q

Quick, Charles, 101, 151

R

Railroads, 35, 52, 53, 131, 173, 174
Recreation Park, 163
Roberson Alonzo, 106
Roebling, W. A., 8
Ross Park, 100
Rounds, J. L., 59
Ruloff, Edward, 68

S

St. John's Ukrainian Orthodox
    Church, 166
St. Mary's Orphan Home, 76
St. Patrick's Church, 43
St. Paul's Episcopal Church, 144
St. Peter and Paul Russian Orthodox
    Church, 165
Security Mutual Building, 125
Serling, Rod, 197
Shapley and Wells, 93
Sisson Brothers and Weldon, 38, 143, 199
South Side Park, 186, 187
Spaulding Bakeries, 150
Spaulding House, 66
State Office Building, 211, 214
State University of New York at
    Binghamton, 201
Stephen's Square, 215
Stickley, Gustav, 118
Stickley-Brandt Furniture, 118
Stone Opera House, 129

Stow Company, 85
Sturdevant-Larrabee, 107, 145, 146
Suspension Bridge, 8
Susquehanna Seminary, 77
Susquehanna Valley Home, 67
Swamp Root, 94

T

Telephones, 114
Television, first broadcast of, 185, 190
Towers, F. B., 32, 33
Triplets, 189
Trolley cars, 81, 132
Tuberculosis Hospital, 96

U

Union, 59

V

Vail-Ballou, 142
Vestal, 59, 75, 133, 134, 198
Veterans Park, 186, 187
Vulcan Corporation, 168

W

Wagener's (White City) Park, 130
Wagon making, 63, 64
Walker's Store, 71
Washington Street Bridge, 88
Watson, Thomas J., 127, 159
Weeds Tannery, 162
Weeks and Dickinson, 183
Whitney, Joshua, 22, 26, 30, 31
Whitney home, 30, 31
Wilkinson Manufacturing, 106
World War I, 127, 144
Wyoming Conference, 145

Y

Your Home Library, 143

About the Author

A native of the area, Gerald R. Smith received his master of arts degree in history from the State University of New York at Binghamton in 1981. Since 1978 he has been an employee of the Broome County Public Library (formerly the Binghamton Public Library) and authored *The People's University: A History of Binghamton Library Societies and the Binghamton Public Library* in 1980.

In 1984 Mayor Juanita Crabb appointed Gerry as Binghamton's city historian, and since that time he has served on that city's sesquicentennial committee, produced a thirty-minute video entitled *Remembrance of Our Past: A History of Binghamton, New York*, been a member of the Imagination Celebration, and acted as project supervisor for the Putnam Collection Preservation Project.

He is currently serving on the board of directors of the Broome County Historical Society, Binghamton's Bicentennial Commission (on the United States Constitution), the Regional Council for Historical Agencies, the Municipal Historians Association of New York State, the American Association for State and Local History, and is a former president of the Broome County Municipal Historians Association.

Views of the local rivers taken in 1890. From Binghamton Illustrated; courtesy Binghamton City Historian